SELLING WITH
CHARISMA

The Sales System Used

—Unwittingly—

By the World's Best Salespeople

Tom Payne

Essential Growth Solutions, LLC

Chicago, Illinois

Selling with Charisma:

The Sales System Used

—Unwittingly—

By the World's Best Salespeople

Book cover design by Christian Fuenfhausen

This book may be ordered online as a paperback or eBook.

Printed in the United States of America.

ISBN 10: 0999507419

ISBN 13: 978-0999507414

Published by: Essential Growth Solutions, LLC

For more information on books by Tom Payne, visit his website: www.tompayne.com

To the people I worked with
in my sales laboratory:

Tess, Erin, Barbara, Carla,
Antonia, Claus and many others

CONTENTS

PART ONE

Understanding Charisma

1

GAME-CHANGING CHARISMA

CHARISMA IN ONE WEEK

Charisma is the difference-making edge possessed by the world's best salespeople, and it can be yours in one week. It will change the way the world perceives you, and when you change how you are perceived you enter a new reality.

I've had clients who were almost invisible to the world around them. Being overlooked was their "reality" until charisma ushered them into a new reality, one where they were magnetic and sought after. Their experience underscores this important fact: How we are perceived affects our ability to influence others and sell in this competitive world, and charisma transforms the way the world sees you in a powerfully favorable way.

Those who express the full power of charisma are rare. Most organizations have only a few top producers, and they stand out in many ways. They have an "it-factor." It is difficult to put into words what that "factor" is, but everyone can see and feel how they have "it," and others don't. However, charisma should not be rare, for it is readily available to all; and if you are in sales you will want to acquire charisma because it will enable you to close sales like the following.

TAKING ON THE SALES-HELL CHALLENGE

I was sitting in my office in our corporate headquarters when the phone rang. It was a call from the COO of a large regional hospital located in the South. He asked to speak to someone in sales, and since all of my sales managers and distributor reps were located in the field, the call came to me.

The COO said, "I need someone from the corporate office to present your nurse call system to my nurses."

I replied, "My Region Manager is the person I need to send your way."

"No sir, no he isn't," the COO replied, "He's been banned from the hospital for life."

"For life?"

"Yes sir. Our nurses hate the guy. Suffice it to say, your company is not too popular with our nursing staff either."

"I'm very sorry to hear that. And I apologize for my Region Manager making such a poor impression."

"Thank you," he replied, "I appreciate the apology. So, can you come on down and make a sales presentation to my nurses?"

"Yes. Of course I can. I'd be happy to."

"Fine. That's good. But I need to prepare you for what you are about to face. Our nurses not only hate your Region Manager, and your company because of him, they also love your competitor. So, this is going to be a tough sell."

Now I was confused. I asked, "Okay, if the nurses hate us, and they love our competitor, then why am I being asked to present to them? Why aren't you buying their system?"

With his folksy, Southern charm he said, "Friend, that's a fair question. You are on our national contract and your competitor is not. Now we can easily buy off-contract whenever we want. However, your contract price is much better than your competitor's list price. And since he's holding aces, he's not feeling the need to offer even a little discount.

"Let me ask you something," he continued, "do you like paying list price?"

"No."

"I'm the same way. So, I thought, 'What the heck. What's the harm in giving your company a shot?' "

"Okay," I continued, still trying to connect all of the dots, "I can understand why *you* want me to present to them. If I close the sale I've saved you and your hospital a tidy sum. But I can't understand why these nurses are willing to sit and listen to my presentation. Based on what you've told me, they hate us and love our competitor."

He said, "You've got that right. They don't want to see you or listen to a thing you say. But I'm the COO, and I'm making them sit and listen to you."

After a pause he added, "Yes sir, like I said, this is going to be a tough sell."

I thought, "And you have a gift for understatement."

THE AMBUSH

They needed to make a quick decision. They would soon be breaking ground on a large, new emergency room expansion, so the COO rounded up the nurses for a presentation that same week. I scheduled a flight and was there a few days after his phone call.

As I was standing in one of their hospital's training rooms with my PowerPoint presentation projected on the screen, the scowling nurses trudged in. Without saying a word they loudly proclaimed, "We'd rather be anywhere than here."

The COO introduced me to the group and asked me to start my presentation. As soon as I opened my mouth, the bugle sounded and the attack was launched. The decision maker jumped up from her seat, got in my face, and launched into a tirade against my Region Manager, my company, and me for having such a derelict Region Manager. She went beyond questioning my integrity; she questioned my competence and sanity. But I listened quietly and respectfully, focusing 100% of my attention on her, nodding my head as I took notes, and waited for her to finish.

Inwardly I smiled as I noted the micro-expressions from her eyes expressing bewilderment. Micro-expressions are those telltale signs that only last an instant and reveal so much. She was puzzled because her ambush was not having its desired effect. I was too calm and confident, and she clearly wanted to rattle me.

As I stood there my facial expression was sober, thoughtful and unafraid. My body language projected how relaxed I was. My tone of voice was respectful, warm and yet authoritative.

At first, the audience thirsted for my blood, but as they saw me calmly stand and receive this merciless tongue-lashing their mood began to change. In sales you learn how to read a room, and this audience was spellbound by this spectacle. They did not know what to make of it.

When she finally ran out of breath and venom I looked directly into the eyes of the assembled nurses throughout the room and said, "All of these points are very important, and I will address each one of them during the course of my presentation. Now let's get started."

I was in control of the situation because of the charisma exercises I practiced prior to this call, ones that I will teach you. I had taken her best shot and had not flinched. Things were not going according to the decision maker's plan; they were following mine.

A REVOLUTIONARY APPROACH

When charisma is added to selling it enables you to make revolutionary changes to your sales approach. You can do what some consider unthinkable and, in this situation, impossible. Midway through the presentation I began talking about their beloved competitor's product and how it was inferior to mine.

Talking about the competitor! This was something I was always taught not to do during my entire sales career. It may be a near-universal sales taboo in America and overseas. When I trained a European salesforce how to use my differentiation techniques one salesperson stood up before the entire class and said, "This might work in America, but it won't work here."

My ideas were too much of a cultural departure for them, and it would take more than one pass to persuade them. But by the end of the course, one of the more charismatic salespeople in attendance decided he would see if differentiation worked.

He later told me, "I was told I had thirty minutes to present to a group of doctors, and that is a lot of time, because they are very busy. But once I started differentiating they became engaged and the presentation lasted two hours." Busy doctors guard their time and receiving two hours from them is not the norm.

His success led other salespeople from Europe to adopt it as well. And guess what? Differentiation worked for them also. But how could it possibly work in this Southern shark tank where I was the chum? After all, even when the customer respects you and your company, you are not supposed to talk about your competitors. Since they disliked me, wouldn't they interrupt me and tell me to stop "bashing" the competition?

Charisma can captivate and enchant. It is almost hypnotic in its power. Consequently, when I was differentiating there were no interruptions from this openly hostile audience, except for the occasional emotional outburst that showed I was turning the tide.

One bearded, burly nurse, who started the presentation glowering at me, blurted out, "The competition's system doesn't have that? Why are we even considering them?"

Later on I heard another say, "We've got to have this system."

These expressions were like emotional eruptions from their subconscious mind. They were automatic, reflex actions that were hot and primal, not cool and rational.

At the end of the hour virtually every person in the room was on my side. Less than a week later we had the purchase order for a system that cost around $250,000 installed. The competitor who was holding aces lost all of his chips.

Before going further let me state that I may not be one of the world's best salespeople, but I have sold with charisma, I've witnessed others sell with it, and I've trained others to sell with it. This perspective enables me to say with confidence, "Charisma is a game-changer. The same words I've used to close sales have utterly failed others who sold without charisma."

IMPLICATIONS

When you think about this situation, and my success within it, it challenges a lot of the conventional wisdom surrounding sales. Let's consider some of the generally accepted sales approaches that I was unable to use even if I wanted to.

Consultative sales: I could not ask these nurses questions, because they would not receive my calls, much less return them. Thus, I could not consult with them to develop a customized proposal. I was flying blind. So, this wiped out "consultative selling" as being the reason why I got their business.

Relationship selling: Well, let's just say my relationship with this group of nurses was strong, but not in a favorable way. So, having a positive relationship, or developing one, was not the basis of my success.

Integrity selling: Ha! I was distrusted. They questioned my integrity because I had such a disreputable Region Manager. This eliminates the possibility of "integrity selling." However, I must emphasize that I was scrupulously honest with them. My sales system depends on such honesty.

Solution selling: If I used "solution selling" in its typical form, then I would have failed. Typically you don't talk about the competitor in this approach. Had I merely presented my solution, they would have bought the competitive product. This is because they believed the competitive system could do the same things our product could. I had to speak about the competition to convince them that they were mistaken.

Finally, I never tried to "close the sale," or ask for the order, and I didn't need to. Their buying decision was made before I left the room, only they didn't know it yet. It would take time before their buying decision—which was subconsciously made—entered their conscious minds. (You'll see how that works in Chapter 3, "The Psychology of Charisma.")

If charisma is so powerful, and so easily acquired, then why doesn't everyone obtain it? The following story answers that question.

THE UNKNOWN ACQUISITION OF CHARISMA

Meet Bob. Bob began developing his charismatic personality at an early age. As a child he observed the way others responded to his smile, his focused attention, and so on. Then, over the course of his life, he adopted these perception-shaping, nonverbal behaviors and developed a charismatic "presence." It made him magnetic and attractive to friends and strangers alike. That most powerful form of communication—nonverbal behavior— was the main source of his charisma, just as it is with everyone else.

This "charismatic face" that Bob showed to the world became an automatic, subconscious expression. It required no conscious thought because it was a part of his nature.

Like the rest of us, Bob rarely thought of his nonverbal behavior or the impact it had on others. He knew he was confident, but was unaware that his confidence was communicated to others. Nor did he realize how the way he spoke with absolute certainty made everyone believe every word he was saying.

Another powerful nonverbal expression was his smile. He knew he had a nice smile, because people occasionally commented on it, but he never knew just how disarming it was to family, friends, and ultimately to customers.

After graduating from college, Bob entered the sales profession and during major sales presentations his charisma was on full display. He radiated a confidence that his customers felt. He projected a sense of authority and was utterly believable. His warmth put them at ease, and they were drawn to his sunny, always positive disposition. Even those customers who distrusted salespeople found themselves captivated by Bob.

As a result, his sales numbers far exceeded everyone else's in the company. Then, when a sales management position opened up, Bob was immediately promoted and an all-too-common scenario played out.

His new boss told him, "Bob, go clone yourself." And Bob tried to do this, but failed. It was an impossible task, because Bob did not know what it was that made him such a great salesperson.

UNWITTINGLY CHARISMATIC

While selling, Bob could not leave his body and look at himself to see his nonverbal behaviors in action. And even if he could see himself selling, perhaps on a videotape, he could not see the impact his nonverbals were having inside his customer's hearts and minds.[1]

Let's say Bob was self-aware enough to realize how charisma fueled his sales success, and he was knowledgeable enough to know that his nonverbals generated charisma. Even if he possessed this degree of understanding, how could he teach others to be charismatic?

After all, nonverbal behavior is, for the most part, a subconscious expression of how we feel. When we feel happy or sad we automatically look happy or sad. We don't have to think about it.

So how do you teach someone to control something that is subconscious? And how do you get someone to adopt these subconscious behaviors that you acquired over the course of your entire life?

Bob failed as a sales manager. The powerful sales approach that he used as a salesperson, the one based on his personal charisma, was used unwittingly. It's one of the main reasons why virtually every top salesperson, who is promoted into sales management, never raises the performance of any of their salespeople to their own level. They can't, because even if they knew what it was that made them so exceptional, they

---

[1] Since the word "nonverbals" does not exist, according to the dictionaries I've checked, allow me to define it and tell you why I use it. "Nonverbals" is simply shorthand for the cumbersome phrase "nonverbal behaviors." I use it to make the ungainly phrase, "nonverbal behaviors," less so.

wouldn't know how to coach others in how to develop subconscious, nonverbal charisma.

Don't worry. It sounds daunting, but it is not. If my clients could acquire charisma in one week, then it cannot be that difficult. Please don't get my assessment of my clients wrong. They were and are great people, but they were going through one of the most difficult times of their life. They had no charisma, and seemingly little hope of acquiring it, but they did in one week.

The power of nonverbal behavior will be made clear in the next chapter, but for now I will simply assert the first of several charisma axioms:

> **Charisma Axiom # 1:** Nonverbal behavior is the primary cause of charisma.

STRATEGY

When I joined Rauland-Borg, the company I worked for in the sales-hell challenge, I was charged with leading a group of Region Managers who covered the U.S. market and were supporting the efforts of our distributor sales force. My strategy was, and is, based on three words: Simplify, focus and achieve.

Simplify: My first task was to learn about all of the opportunities my sales organization faced, and then simplify this mass of data into a solution that focused on the single most important driver of sales growth.

Focus: By focusing all of my energy on one thing, the most important thing, I had far better odds of succeeding than if I had tried to focus on three or four things.

Achieve: Once I found this driver of growth I focused virtually all of my attention and energy on it until we achieved dramatic sales growth.

FINDING THE MOST IMPORTANT DRIVER OF GROWTH

To discover this driver of growth I asked virtually everyone, "What is it?" and got a variety of answers. As it turned out, no one knew. But after two months of research I discovered it: Sales training.

Here is why it was more important than anything else. We were selling through distributor sales representatives of varying quality. Where we had good distributor sales reps we did well. Where we had bad distributor sales reps we did poorly. The quality of my Region Managers was not the primary issue. My best Region Managers were not very successful when a bad distributor sales rep was involved in the sale.

Part of our problem was this: Our distributor reps, many from small markets with small talent pools, were competing against polished, direct sales reps from multi-billion dollar competitors who were known throughout the world: GE, Tyco, and Hill-Rom.

This name recognition was a huge advantage for them, because Rauland was virtually unknown. Imagine this: Early in my tenure with Rauland I once presented to a large Chicago-based hospital system. It was opening a new children's hospital that was located within thirty miles of our corporate headquarters. As I was presenting the key decision maker asked, "If you are about the same size as Hill-Rom and GE in the nurse call market, then why have we never heard of you?"

Even in our hometown we were unknown.

Another significant obstacle our distributor reps faced was this: The majority had never received a day of sales training before. To help our distributor reps compete I developed a weeklong sales training course focusing on the verbal elements of charisma: Differentiation, stories, asking effective questions, etc. Verbal charisma is very powerful and the results far exceeded my expectations. By the time I left Rauland we were market dominant, possessing more than 50% of the nurse call market.

EFFECTIVE BUT LACKING IN NONVERBAL CHARISMA

As powerful as verbal charisma is, nonverbal charisma is even more powerful, and my program did not include training in how to become nonverbally charismatic. This sometimes made techniques, like differentiation, work against my sales trainees. For example, one of my trainees tried to differentiate in a far less difficult situation than the sales-hell challenge, and it blew up in her face. A nurse accused her of bashing the competition and told her she needed to stop doing this right now.

A few days after she scolded my trainee, I then presented to this same nurse and talked about the competition repeatedly without any objections. Nonverbal charisma—the missing ingredient—made what I said satisfying, and its absence made what the trainee said unpleasant. The words were virtually identical (I'd taught her what to say!), but the end results were as different as a purchase order and a rejection notice. Not only did the scolding nurse listen peacefully to my differentiation message, her hospital gave us a PO. (We will revisit this sales situation in greater detail.)

I failed to include nonverbal charisma in my sales training program because, like Bob in the above story, I was "unwittingly" charismatic. The next chapter will explain, more comprehensively, why charisma is so hidden from our sight.

Now, before closing this chapter, I will share the organizing principle of my original sales training course. It is still the organizing principle and it helps explain the selling power of charisma.

FOR EVERY CAUSE THERE IS AN EFFECT, FOR EVERY EFFECT THERE IS A CAUSE

As I developed my sales training course I was forced to think deeply about fundamental questions that I'd never considered. Perhaps the most crucial question was, "What causes a customer's buying decision?"

Until we know what *causes* the buying-decision-*effect* how can we intentionally cause it? Ignorance of these causes makes our sales success accidental instead of intentional. We are like people throwing everything against a wall in the hope that something sticks. So, we end up trying an assortment of ideas, and are confused when these techniques work sometimes and other times fail.

To answer the question, "What causes the buying decision?" my thought process went down this path:

> Buying decisions are made in the mind. Therefore, what are the primary psychological influences on our decision-making process?

I came up with two very large influences: Reason and emotion, or rationality and feelings. I then wondered whether the buying decision was more head or more heart. Which influence predominated?

After much study I concluded that emotions cause the buying decision, not reason. Some of my research from back then now follows.

Economists developed the Consumer Sentiment Index to predict buying behavior. It measures the consumer's feelings about the economy and about their own situation. Are they optimistic (likely buyers) or pessimistic (probably not in a spending mood)? These emotions are predictive of buying behavior, and note how there is no Consumer Rationality Index.

The history of sales produced revealing statements like, "Nobody ever got fired for buying IBM." This notion took root during the days of IBM's mainframe dominance. Mainframes were expensive investments for companies to make forty to sixty years ago, and people bought the costlier

IBM mainframe because they knew it would work. If you spent tons of money to buy a mainframe that failed, then you would have committed a much-dreaded CLM (career-limiting move). IT Directors feared this outcome and this led to the saying, "Nobody ever got fired for buying IBM."

Think about it. The typically rational people in IT departments were making a buying decision based, in part, on the emotion of fear.

MONEY IS EMOTION QUANTIFIED

Finally, the emotional power of money affects every buying decision and the following illustrates how money's emotional power increases as the dollar amount rises.

If you loan a good friend a dollar and they don't pay it back, big deal. It is not enough money to get worked up over. But if you loan a good friend $500, and they fail to pay it back, then it can end the relationship.

> More than half of consumers have seen a friendship end over money owed.
>
> ...Nearly three-quarters say their financial breaking point is $500 or less.[2]

As the dollar amount increased so did the intensity of the emotional response to being stiffed. This is because money is emotion quantified. Or, another way of putting it: The more money, the more emotion.

The emotional nature of money has the following impact on sales. The more money involved in securing your product or service, the greater the influence emotion has over the buying decision. Again, "Nobody ever got fired for buying IBM." It was a high-dollar buying decision and it was emotionally caused.

One of my favorite demonstrations of the emotional nature of high-dollar purchasing decisions was a video I would show sales teams that was designed to sell the Bugatti Veyron, a >$2,000,000 sports car. It showed the Veyron speeding across a remote stretch of highway to the tune of a pulsing sound track, and it failed to use one word. Words and statistics might convey a logical argument, but what logical argument supports spending that amount of money on a car? So, the pitch was purely emotional: The more money, the more emotion.

---

[2] Bank of America, 2017, Friends Again Report.

This money-emotion connection holds true when you look at the world of low-priced commodities. Emotion plays a much smaller role in these buying decisions. The objective logic of price rules the day. Which product is cheaper and of acceptable quality?

Yet, even here emotion influences the buying decision to a degree. A charismatic salesperson will have more success selling commodity products than one who lacks this attractive, emotion-generating power. People still prefer to buy from people they like, or are drawn toward.

EMPLOYING THE EMOTIONAL CAUSES

Until we tailor our sales approach to apply the emotional causes of the buying-decision-effect, we will fail to close sales consistently. That is what I taught salespeople to do in my training program, and it worked.

However, my solution was incomplete. It failed to give them nonverbal charisma, the emotional language of the subconscious mind that changes the way a person is perceived and impacts the power of the message they are delivering.

That may not sound important at first, but imagine if you had the power to generate feelings toward you like trust, likability, and confidence. It would make your customer want to do business with you, believe what you are saying, and this would affect how they perceive your product offering.

In my sales-hell scenario, my charisma imbued me with so much authority that no one challenged me, or anything I said, while I was calmly, surgically dissecting their beloved competitor's product.

The bottom line: Charisma tilts the playing field in your favor.

The more we understand about charisma, the more we will want to wield its influence. In the next chapter we will look at the power plant of charisma—nonverbal behaviors—and continue to explore why this ability to charm and enchant is so powerful in sales.

2

THE POWER OF
NONVERBAL BEHAVIOR

"ALL THE WORLD'S A STAGE, AND ALL THE MEN AND WOMEN MERELY PLAYERS"[1]

Nonverbal behavior is our most powerful form of communication and when we sell we are communicating. Therefore, we are not selling as powerfully as we should until we master nonverbal communication.

To illustrate the power of nonverbals, let's look at a profession that requires nonverbal mastery: Acting. When an actor plays in a sad scene, he must express this sadness nonverbally. If he cannot express his role's emotions nonverbally, then he will soon be out of work.

Actors are masters of this most powerful form of communication, and this explains why so many people are drawn to them. They have that mysterious "it" factor. Their nonverbal mastery makes them so charismatic that people become star-struck in their presence. It doesn't matter that they are, in some instances, not all that good looking, stupid, narcissistic, unethical and as boring as an oatmeal diet; people will still follow them. They are living proof that charisma can make some of the most unpromising people magnetic and enchanting.

---

[1] William Shakespeare, *As You Like It*, Act II, Scene VII.

This connection between nonverbal behavior and charisma—which will be strengthened in the following pages—produces our next axiom:

> **Charisma Axiom # 2:** Charisma is acquired by those who master their nonverbal voice.

Imagine having the charismatic impact of a movie star on your customers. Start mastering your nonverbal voice and you are on your way.

THE POWER OF NONVERBAL BEHAVIOR

One of the purposes of nonverbal behaviors is this: They reinforce and strengthen what our words are trying to communicate. We see this in the following encounter.

Imagine a life coach holding his client's gaze, and saying with an authoritative tone that rings with conviction: "I believe in you! You can do this! You've done it before!"

The client would likely respond, "He's right. I have done it before. I can do it!"

This life coach's words and his nonverbal behaviors communicate the same message of encouragement. He is speaking with an authentic, influential voice, and it has the power to give confidence to a person struggling with self-doubt.

However, when our words say one thing and our nonverbals say another, we are speaking with an inauthentic voice. This can make our words communicate the opposite of what we intend.

For example, consider a different life coach who says with a flat, lifeless tone, a blank facial expression and no eye contact, "I believe in you. You can do this. You've done it before."

His client would probably think, "I don't believe a word he is saying, because he doesn't seem to believe it. Wow! Nobody believes in me. Not even my life coach. I'm an even bigger loser than I thought."

One coach inspired and encouraged his client, while the other coach increased his client's self-doubt. Both coaches used the exact same words, but they had the opposite effect. The difference maker in their ability to persuade, influence, and sell—if you will—was their nonverbal charisma.

We have just dipped our toe in the waters of nonverbal behavior and already we are seeing how they can influence others. They give us the power to charm, enchant and persuade, and this leads to our third axiom:

Charisma Axiom # 3: Charismatic people have an authentic voice. Their words and nonverbal behaviors say the same thing.

Imagine the impact of an authentic or an inauthentic voice during a sales presentation. If your voice doesn't ring with conviction, and your face doesn't radiate confidence, but your competitor's nonverbal behaviors do, then who will the customer believe and buy from? They likely will buy from the person they trust, like and believe in, and that person is the one who presented a solution to them with an authentic, charismatic voice.

WORDS OR NONVERBALS: WHAT DO YOU BELIEVE?

When our nonverbals and our words communicate different messages, which message is believed? According to Dr. Albert Mehrabian, our words account for 7% of personal communication, while our tone of voice accounts for 38%, and our body language (which includes facial expression) accounts for 55%.

These percentages were applied to communications involving emotion and attitude, and "selling" is a type of communication that certainly involves emotion. That is because it involves money—emotion quantified—so these stats, if accurate, would apply. Again, if these stats are real, then nonverbals account for 93% of the message being heard. So, when our words say one thing and our nonverbals say another, customers tend to believe the nonverbal message.

Even if Dr. Merhabian got the percentages wrong, the gist of his message is backed up by our own experience. Have you ever been in the presence of a depressed person? A person who feels depressed will look depressed. And if he tells you, "I feel okay," do you believe him? No. His words are discounted. You believe what his nonverbals are communicating and surmise, "Obviously he is trying to mask feelings he doesn't want to discuss." And this leads to our fourth axiom:

Charisma Axiom # 4: When our words say one thing, but our nonverbal behaviors say another, people tend to believe our nonverbal voice.

To acquire charisma we must gain control of our nonverbal voice because, as the above percentages show, it is our most powerful way of communicating to our customers.

A WORKING DEFINITION

Accurately defining nonverbal behavior was a critical step in my development of a system to control it. My working definition was:

> Nonverbal behaviors are, for the most part, automatic, subconscious expressions of our physical, emotional and mental state (PEM state).

Let's briefly analyze this definition to see if it holds up to scrutiny.

Is nonverbal behavior a subconscious expression of our physical state?

> Yes. If you are bone-tired, then your listless body language and weary tone of voice will automatically communicate your exhaustion. You will not have to think, "Since I'm running on fumes I need to express my exhaustion nonverbally." No conscious thought is required. We automatically express our physical state— exhaustion, vitality, etc.—nonverbally.

Nonverbal behavior is also a subconscious expression of our emotional state as is evidenced by the example of the depressed person, and the same holds true for the happy person. If someone feels happy it shows.

Finally, nonverbal behavior automatically expresses our mental state:

> If your mental state is characterized by confusion and an inability to focus, then you will look confused and scatterbrained. No one wants to look this way. So, when a confused person tries to hide their confusion by saying, "Of course I understand," they are often asked, "Are you sure you got that? Do you want me to go over it again?" Their confusion is written all over their face, and this expression required no conscious thought on their part. It occurred subconsciously and automatically.

CONSCIOUS CONTROL OF NONVERBAL BEHAVIOR

In my working definition I wrote, "Nonverbal behaviors are, *for the most part*, automatic, subconscious expressions...." I added the phrase, "for the most part," because it is possible to control nonverbal behavior consciously, and even change it over time.

The U.S. Army proves this every year. A soldier slouches at boot camp and a drill instructor yells in his face, "Stand up straight!" The slouching soldier springs to a position of attention. It is a conscious response. And if reinforced often enough, this erect posture enters the soldier's subconscious mind in the form of a new habit.

This ability to reprogram the subconscious mind and produce a desired type of nonverbal behavior is important. *Part Two* of this book will show you how to reprogram it faster than what takes place at a boot camp, and without a barking drill sergeant.

THE LIMITATIONS OF CONSCIOUS CONTROL

We can consciously control nonverbal behavior, but most people cannot do so over extended periods of time. This is due to the conscious mind's limited bandwidth.

To illustrate this difficulty, let's say you are giving a sales presentation and someone interrupts you to ask a question. You now have to listen to what he is asking, decode his message, determine if there is a meta-communication—e.g., does his question reveal a hidden agenda—formulate a clear, well-worded reply, deliver the response, and make sure your tone of voice is confident, that you are standing tall yet looking relaxed, and your facial expression is warm and approachable, yet authoritative. That is more cognitive load than the conscious mind can bear. Then, absent conscious control, our nonverbal behaviors revert to being automatic, subconscious expressions of our PEM state.

Perhaps the most useful thing my definition of nonverbal behavior accomplished was to help me see how to control them. Since they are a subconscious expression of our PEM state, then one of the most effective ways to control them is through controlling our PEM state. Again, *Part Two* will cover this subject.

BEHIND THE POWER OF NONVERBAL BEHAVIOR

What is it that makes nonverbal behavior powerful enough to produce charisma and influence buying decisions?

Part of its power comes from our mirror neuron system (MNS). The MNS is a fairly recent discovery dating from the 1980s and 1990s. It is:

> The "I feel what you feel" emotional empathy system.

Gets in sync with others' emotions by reading *facial expressions* and interpreting *tone of voice* and other *nonverbal emotional cues*.[2]

Think about that for a moment: Our brains are wired to feel what others feel, and this feeling is based on their nonverbal communication. This means we have the ability to communicate our emotional state to another person during face-to-face talk. If we feel great, then our nonverbal behaviors will express this, and those with whom we interact will feel great too, because they feel what we feel.

You have probably felt the joy of a person who has just heard great news. Their joy makes you smile. He communicated his ecstasy and delight to your emotional empathy system through his nonverbal expressions, and it all took place automatically and subconsciously. You did not consciously think, "This person is overjoyed. I need to feel over-the moon to express solidarity with him."

Whatever the emotion, we subconsciously interpret, and automatically respond, to someone's nonverbal behaviors. Our brains are wired to do this, and the charismatic potential of this is obvious. For if you optimize your PEM state, and become a fountain of positive energy, then you will be magnetic. People are attracted to the glow of another's positive emotions, and want to be around those people who express them.

You might be thinking, "That sounds exhausting! How could I maintain that act?" Rest assured that the charisma produced by these exercises is effortless, automatic and, when engaging in face-to-face talk, it requires no acting or conscious exertion. If it did, then it would not work.

THE MYSTERY OF CHARISMA

This explains why charisma is clothed in mystery:

A charismatic person speaks and communicates his charisma through subconsciously generated nonverbal behaviors. Meanwhile, the listening person's subconscious mind responds to these nonverbals by automatically feeling the feeling they communicate.

What we have here is the subconscious mind of one person communicating to the subconscious mind of another. No wonder charisma is mysterious!

---

[2] Louann Brizendine, MD, *The Male Brain* (New York: Harmony Books, 2010), p. xvi. Emphasis mine.

This also explains the "unwitting" use of charisma by the world's top salespeople. It is difficult to become aware of, much less understand, something that operates subconsciously for both the salesperson and the customer. Not to mention the fact that most charismatic salespeople developed these subconscious expressions of confidence and warmth, authority and kindness, over the course of their lives. They are almost certainly aware of the impact they personally have on other people, but are probably unaware that this power to influence others is largely due to their nonverbal behavior.

SALES IMPLICATIONS

My original sales training course focused on the emotional aspects of verbal behavior, the words we speak during a presentation, and it was able to drive amazing sales results.

In retrospect, this is somewhat surprising, because the buying decision is emotionally made and the spoken word is the preferred communication vehicle of the rational, conscious mind. This connection of words and rationality is captured by the Greek word "logos." It is a word that is typically translated as either "word" or "reason." "Logos" is the root word of logic. And as we will see in the next chapter, the more emotional, subconscious mind does not communicate to us through the medium of words. It is why the commercial for the Bugatti Veyron was wordless. The last thing the makers of this car wanted was to engage the consumer's rational mind.

Also in the next chapter, we will see how the consciously made buying decision is emotionally driven by the subconscious mind. If this is true, then we need to learn the subconscious, emotional language of nonverbal behavior, because it is even more powerful than the words we say.

This is what Dr. Mehrabian's research strongly suggested. It poses the question: Do we want to speak with 7% of our voice, or 100% of it?

The assertion that a conscious buying decision is caused by a subconscious process might sound ridiculous. But hopefully it will make sense after we explore the psychology of charisma and decision-making in the next chapter.

3

THE PSYCHOLOGY OF CHARISMA

"I'M OF TWO MINDS ABOUT THIS SUBJECT."

We begin to understand the psychology of charisma by understanding the interaction of our two minds that act as one. We have a lightning-fast subconscious mind and a slower, more deliberate conscious, rational mind. There is a dramatic difference in speed between these two systems. According to one researcher, the adaptive unconscious—his preferred term—processes 11,000,000 bits of sensory data per second, while the rational mind processes about 40 bits per second.[1] As the note below indicates, the vast majority of these bits are visual and that will have sales implications that we will explore in a moment.

Researchers often call this subconscious mind "System 1," and they settle on this strange name because it is less limiting than other commonly used options. The more descriptive names, used by others, reveal important insights into System 1, but they can also put it in a box. Since we are just beginning to understand its operation, this name—System 1—is helpful because it does not steer our thinking in just one direction. But since the more descriptive names reveal insights, let's take a look at them to gain a better understanding of the way System 1 operates.

---

[1] "Scientists have determined this number [11,000,000—my note] by counting the receptor cells each sense organ has and the nerves that go from these cells to the brain. Our eyes alone receive and send over 10,000,000 signals to our brains each second." Timothy D. Wilson, *Strangers to Ourselves: Discovering the Adaptive Unconscious* (Cambridge, MA: Belknap Press of Harvard University Press, 2002), p. 24.

MEANINGFUL NAMES

One of the insightful names for System 1 is the *emotional unconscious*, calling attention to its emotional nature. Since the buying decision is largely caused by emotion and not reason, this name alone tells us the powerful role System 1 likely plays in buying decisions.

Others call it the *cognitive unconscious* to indicate the way this mind is performing cognitive functions beneath the surface of our awareness. In other words, System 1 is not merely a passive repository of memories, traumas, etc. It is an active mind that can and does operate independently of conscious control.

Finally, some prefer to call System 1 the *adaptive unconscious* to highlight the way our subconscious mind has adapted over evolutionary time to preserve our species, among other activities. Self-preservation is one of System 1's most important roles, and to ensure it performs this role well, it never sleeps. It is a tireless sentry scanning the horizon for threats, and when it spots one it springs into action immediately.

We see this independent activity of System 1 in the "fight-flight-freeze" response. For example, you are walking along a path in the woods and spot a long, thin black object lying on the ground across your path. You feel this surge of alarm throughout your body—that is how System 1 communicates, because it does not use words—and you stop dead in your tracks. This was not a consciously arrived at decision. It was automatically made and did not involve reason. But now System 2, the rational-conscious mind, gets involved, analyzes the object and determines it is not a snake but a stick, and you continue walking.

System 1 did not wait for System 2's authorization, because the rational-conscious mind was and is too slow, but the two systems did work in partnership. This same sort of partnership occurs in decision-making, and since sales is the art of causing a buying decision it helps to understand how these systems move us toward decisions.

PICK A CARD, ANY CARD

The role System 1 plays in our decision-making is immense, as the following experiment shows. It involved two red decks of cards and two blue decks. To the experimental subjects they were just four decks of cards, however, picking a card from the different colored decks produced different outcomes. The red decks delivered big gains, but bigger losses. The blue decks delivered small gains but smaller losses. The net effect was you eventually ended up losing with the red decks and gaining with the blue.

Thus, there was a problem with the red decks. We would expect lightning-fast System 1, scanning the horizon for threats, to spot this pattern before slower System 2, and then warn the conscious mind about the problem through feelings of unease toward the red decks. But how fast would it spot the threat—losing money—and how long would it take before this information became conscious?

The experiment's subjects had a gut feeling that there was a problem with the red decks around the drawing of the fiftieth card. A subconscious intuition had entered the realm of the conscious mind, but this dim awareness was not a fully articulated thought. They could not put the red deck's problem into words. They simply knew there was a problem. Then, around card eighty, they knew exactly what was wrong with the red decks and put it into words.

When did System 1 figure this out? To answer that we return to how it communicates its concerns to us.

THE EMOTIONAL LANGUAGE OF THE BODY

As previously stated, System 1 communicates through the body, through gut feelings and intuitions. When System 1 detects a threat, it prepares the body for action by initiating the fight-flight-freeze response, and this response can be physiologically monitored and measured:

> This fight-or-flight reaction is not all or nothing; it operates on a continuum. …And part of these continuous autonomic reactions to experience is microsweating: Your whole body, including your palms, becomes damper or dryer in proportion to any upticks or downticks in your level of emotional arousal at any given moment.
>
> This is good news for us scientists because it means we can measure your emotional reaction to the things you see by simply monitoring the degree of your microsweating.[2]

We return to the experiment using the red and blue cards. The experimenters used microsweating to determine the timing of System 1's emotional response to the threat posed by the red decks. This response occurred, along with an accelerated heart rate, at card ten.

---

[2] V.S. Ramachandran, *The Tell-Tale Brain: A Neuroscientist's Quest for What Makes Us Human* (New York: W. W. Norton & Company, Inc., 2011), p. 70.

This prompts a question: If System 1 recognized the threat around card ten, then why did it take so long—forty cards—before System 2 was dimly aware of the threat the red decks posed? That seems like an awfully long lag-time if this "adaptive" unconscious mind of ours is really interested in communicating threats and protecting us.

System 1 was not asleep at the wheel during that forty-card progress to a gut feeling. It was affecting the conscious choices of System 2 long before the experimental subjects became aware of their gut feeling. After System 1 saw the threat posed by the red cards, it began steering the subjects away from making red-card choices. Conscious decisions were being influenced by non-conscious information and the experimental subjects were completely unaware of this.

NONCONSCIOUS INFORMATION AND PERCEPTION

Nonconscious information can influence our decision-making as well as our perception of others, and our feelings toward them, as the next experiment shows.

John Bargh and Paula Pietromonaco asked the subjects in their experiment to tell them if the flash on the computer screen came from the right or left of the screen. This was an easy task. But what the subjects did not know was the flash contained a word. Though their conscious mind was unaware of the appearance of this word, System 1 saw it and responded.

The experiment involved one group being exposed to flashes containing words related to hostility, such as "insult," "unkind," etc. Another group was exposed to words that were unrelated to hostility.

> Next, people took part in what they thought was an unrelated experiment on how people form impressions of others. They read a paragraph describing a man named Donald, who acted in somewhat ambiguous ways that might be construed as hostile, such as, "A salesman knocked at the door, but Donald refused to let him enter."
>
> Those who had seen flashes of hostile words judged Donald to be more hostile and unfriendly than did people who had not seen the flashes of hostile words....[3]

In the above experiment, System 2 did not come to its conclusions independently. Non-conscious information, lodged in System 1, shaped

---

[3] Timothy D. Wilson, p. 30.

conscious perception and conclusions. This influence led Daniel Kahneman, a winner of the Nobel Prize in economics, to characterize System 1's impact on System 2's decision making as follows:

> System 1 effortlessly originates "impressions and feelings that are the main sources of the …deliberate choices of System 2."[4]

If we would cause System 2's "deliberate choices," then we need to influence the "impressions and feelings" of System 1 that are the main source of these choices. This is one of the reasons why nonverbal charisma is so powerful. It makes these "impressions," and stirs these "feelings," that influence the "deliberate choices" that include buying decisions. It speaks the emotional language of the emotional unconscious, or System 1.

INSTANTANEOUS ASSESSMENTS

The following research shows how System 1 makes assessments of important personality traits based purely on nonverbal behavior in one second. Subjects, in Dr. Alexander Todorov's experiment, looked at side-by-side photos of the faces of two different people.

The subjects did not know it but they were looking at the faces of people who ran against each other in past elections for the U.S. Senate and the House of Representatives (in 2000, 2002). One headshot was the picture of the winner and the other was the loser. They were also showed photos of Senate and House candidates who were running against each other in elections yet to take place (in 2004).

They only had one second to view the two faces and answer the question, "Which person is more competent?" And to encourage their reliance on System 1, the subjects were told to work as quickly as possible and follow their "gut instincts."

The reason why the researchers chose the variable "competence" was because, "Competence emerges as one of the most important trait attributes on which people evaluate politicians."[5] It needed to be an important "trait attribute," because of what they were trying to predict:

> a) Would the person who looked more competent be the winner of a past election (in 2000 or 2002)?

---

[4] Kahneman, p. 21.
[5] Alexander Todorov, Anesu N. Mandisodza, Amir Goren, Crystal C. Hall (2005) *Inferences of Competence from Faces Predict Election Outcomes* Science. Vol 308, 10 June 2005, p. 1624.

b) And would those more competent-looking people, who were actively campaigning, go on to win in the coming election (2004)?

The results were as follows: "...the candidate who was perceived as more competent won in 71.6% of the Senate races and in 66.8% of the House races."[6] This accuracy applied to those candidates who were elected in the past and those who would soon be elected in the future.

How we are assessed, and how we assess others, is a System 1 operation that takes seconds, or perhaps a split-second in some cases. This instantaneous assessment relies heavily on nonverbal behaviors, with facial expression being one of the most important cues.

Now imagine if your facial expression communicates you are more competent, or less competent, than your competitor. Would this affect the vote the customers cast when they make a buying decision? How could it not?

But do not think that System 1 is limited to forming judgments on just one variable of our personality. In another experiment students watched thirty seconds of videotape of a professor teaching a class. There was no sound track. Based on this limited, visual, nonverbal behavior, they were asked to rate these instructors on attributes such as confidence, enthusiasm, optimism, likability and warmth on a scale from one to nine.

The actual students of the videotaped teachers, who had a semester's worth of observing him or her in person, were also asked to rate him or her on these same attributes. The evaluations of the two groups were significantly correlated on nine of the fifteen measures.[7] When the videotape was shortened to fifteen seconds, and later to only six seconds, the correlation between the two groups remained high.[8]

These "significantly correlated" nine traits are closely aligned with the dimensions of charisma that we will study in Chapter 5. The strength dimension is reflected in the traits "confident," "competent" and

---

[6] Todorov, et al., p. 1624.

[7] The following nine traits were highly correlated: Optimistic .84, Confident .82, Dominant .79, Active .77, Enthusiastic .76, Likable .73, Warm .67, Competent .56, Supportive .55. The other six traits were less so: Professional .53, Accepting .50, Attentive .48, Empathetic .45, Honest .32, (Not) anxious .26. As can be seen, four of the six traits that failed to make the statistical cut were still within ten points of the "Supportive" trait that did.

[8] This research appeared in: *Ambady, N., & Rosenthal, R. (1993). Half a minute: Predicting teacher evaluations from thin slices of nonverbal behavior and physical attractiveness. Journal of Personality and Social Psychology, 64(3), 431-441.*

"dominant." The warmth dimension is captured by traits like "likable," "warm," and "supportive." And on the energy dimension there is "optimism," "active" and "enthusiastic."

Understanding the dimensions of charisma is vital to balancing it, for if it leans too far in one direction it can become repellent instead of attractive.

To cause a buying decision we are trying to employ those tactics and techniques that generate favorable emotions. We are also trying to avoid creating a mental state in our customer's mind that works against us. One such state is called "cognitive strain."

COGNITIVE EASE AND COGNITIVE STRAIN

The operation of System 1 is virtually effortless and automatic. On the other hand, System 2 requires effort. It will labor over a complex math problem and solve it. System 1 is not able to solve complex math problems, or operate in a rational way.

When System 2 is resting, not solving problems or attending to some potential threat, it is in a state of cognitive ease. This is where we want our customer's minds to be when we are selling. It is an accepting frame of mind, characterized by trust and belief.

Kahneman contrasted the two mental states as follows:

> When you are in a state of cognitive ease, you are probably in a good mood, like what you see, *believe what you hear,* trust your intuitions, and feel that the current situation is comfortably familiar. You are also likely to be relatively casual and superficial in your thinking. When you feel strained you are *more likely to be vigilant and suspicious,* invest more effort in what you are doing, feel less comfortable....[9]

We do not want our customers "to be vigilant and suspicious." We want them to "believe what [they] hear." This means we need to avoid causing cognitive strain, and there are several ways to achieve this.

---

[9] Daniel Kahneman, *Thinking, Fast and Slow* (New York: Farrar, Straus and Giroux, 2011), p. 60. Emphasis mine.

SIMPLICITY

One way to avoid cognitive strain is to make our sales presentations simple and easy to understand. If we use big words and make unnecessarily complex arguments, then System 2 is called into action to make sense of what we are saying.

Our presentations needs to be graphic—pictures must dominate—instead of text-laden. If you've ever had to sit through a PowerPoint presentation that showed one text-crammed slide after another, then you know what the phrase "death-by-PowerPoint" means. This presentation style generates cognitive strain and makes people "feel less comfortable." That is not a good way to generate the emotions that cause buying decisions.

When I've analyzed presentations in the past I've often turned one data-dumping slide into five slides with images to make the data—if it was worthwhile—easier to understand. Too much data activates System 2 and forces it to work too hard. It is trying to decipher the wall of text. If this cognitive strain continues for too long, or becomes too intense, it will cause the customer's mind to disengage and shut down. They're worn out. Therefore, sales presentations need to be simple, clear and digestible.

AUTHENTICITY

We need to speak with an authentic voice to keep cognitive strain far away. Our words and nonverbals need to say the same thing, for when they don't a customer's System 1 immediately picks up on this and alerts his rational-conscious mind that it needs to investigate. It poses the question, "Why are his nonverbals saying one thing while his words say another? His words are confident and strong, but his tone is shaky and he seems very nervous and unsure of himself." This cognitive strain can result in the customer not believing a word we are saying.

THE VISUAL BRAIN

Another thing that makes nonverbal behavior such a powerful way of communicating is the way so much of it is visual and our brains are primarily oriented to sight above all of the other senses. As Dr. John Medina notes:

> Visual processing doesn't just assist in the perception of our world. It dominates the perception of our world.

> If you think the brain has to devote to vision a lot of its precious thinking resources, you are right on the money. Visual processing takes up about half of everything your brain does, in fact.[10]

Dr. Medina claims the visual sense dominates all of the other senses. But what about wine experts, people with highly developed senses of smell and taste? Surely their acute senses would not be dominated by their sense of sight.

There are millions of wine aficionados, but genuine wine experts are far fewer in number. Where would a researcher go to find a large enough sampling for an experiment? The premier, wine-producing regions are where many of these experts tend to gather, and that is where the following experiment took place:

> In 2001 the University of Bordeaux's Frederick Brochet presented fifty-four wine experts with two glasses of wine, one red and one white. They were asked to taste and describe them. After drinking the red wine they described it as being "jammy," and spoke about its crushed red fruit.

> That seems like a reasonable description, except for the fact that both glasses of wine came from the same bottle of white wine. Their glass of "red" wine was actually a white wine that had been colored by a flavorless, red dye. Their visual brains overpowered their highly developed senses of smell and taste. Their brain tasted a red wine because it saw a red wine.

When we are presenting to our customers they are listening to the words we say, but more importantly they are subconsciously observing our nonverbal behaviors, or the way we say it. These behaviors are like the flavorless dye that makes a white wine taste red. They color everything we do or say—the way we are perceived—for better or for worse.

THE PICTORIAL SUPERIORITY EFFECT

We have visual brains that can do extraordinary things with the massive amount of visual information we store away and access. One of these capabilities is called the pictorial superiority effect. It is one of the reasons why any presentation should be dominated by pictures instead of text:

---

[10] John Medina, *Brain Rules* (Seattle: Pear Press, 2014), pp. 183, 189. This is another great read if you are interested in how the mind works.

The pictorial superiority effect is truly Olympian. Tests performed years ago showed that people could remember more than 2,500 pictures with at least 90 percent accuracy several days later, even though subjects saw each picture for about ten seconds.[11]

That is remarkable, but imagine how our minds respond to images that are associated with threat (like an angry face), or safety (a friendly, smiling face). System 1 maintains our model of the world and in it is a catalogue of these faces. When an angry person is approaching you do not have to consciously piece together that he is angry. There is no rational assessment that goes like this: He has a red face, a snarl, he is emitting a growling sound, hmm, I think he's angry. No, you know it immediately.

Nonverbal behavior is what our visual brains were designed to assess in microseconds. There is survival value in being able to interpret whether a strange person walking toward us is a potential friend or foe.

SUBCONSCIOUS DECISION MAKING IN THE REAL WORLD

We've seen this subconscious, decision-making process play out in the real world of "sales" in the following way.

Whether a job interviewee has any sales ability or not, he must sell himself. The interviewer, or buyer, must make a hiring decision. As with buying an expensive product, the hiring decision is an emotion-laden investment that involves risk. The person he hires could be a bad fit who totally disrupts team chemistry and gets paid a lot of money to do so.

In this high-pressure sales situation, job interviewers often report that they make a hiring decision at around the fifteen-minute mark, and many people are surprised that these important decisions are made so quickly. But I believe they are made much sooner. The fifteen-minute mark is like the red deck's fiftieth card. It's the "gut-feeling-has-entered-my-consciousness" phase.

At fifteen minutes the hiring authority has a sense that this person is, or is not, the one. But long before that, through an almost instantaneous assessment of nonverbal behaviors, System 1 quickly came to its own conclusion. After about the first minute the interviewer is at card ten, because it takes seconds for System 1 to conclude, "This person looks confident, trustworthy, likable and competent. Hire this person." It then takes fifteen minutes for this gut feeling to enter his consciousness.

---

[11] Medina, p. 191.

The nonconscious information of nonverbal behavior is shaping the way the hiring authority perceives the interviewee. And based on my extensive experience with coaching job interviewees, I believe nonverbal behavior is the primary cause of hiring decisions.[12]

If my hypothesis is correct, then this solves a mystery. Namely, why is it that hiring authorities are almost always unable to explain why they did not hire someone? The reasons they give are uniformly lame, or so general that they are virtually meaningless. They cannot offer meaningful, rational answers, because the decision was subconsciously made for emotional, non-rational reasons.

I imagine some may disagree with the claim I am making about the outsized impact of nonverbal behavior on the hiring decision, but defer judgment until you meet some of the people who gained mastery of their nonverbal voice in the next chapter. They are the people to whom this book is dedicated, the courageous and determined jobseekers who were part of my sales laboratory.

MY SALES LABORATORY

As I mentioned, I had no idea I had charisma, or that it was a critical element in my sales success. So, how did I finally stumble upon this subconscious selling power? It happened while I was working with jobseekers and witnessed the results that my nonverbal training program was generating. One after another, these candidates became undeniably charismatic.

Why did I focus on training them on ways to control their nonverbal behavior, if I did not know how critical it was? I focused on nonverbals because many of these jobseekers were so beaten down by the grueling job search process that their bad nonverbal behaviors were painfully obvious. Some had a hangdog, defeated look that made you think, "I wouldn't hire this guy either." So I knew I needed to do something about their nonverbals if they were to have a shot at being hired.

Fortunately, I had a solution. It was based on exercises I used to change my own nonverbal behavior many years ago, and that I continued to use throughout my sales career. They worked well, particularly in large,

---

[12] I've literally coached thousands of jobseekers in the art of interviewing through radio podcasts, live radio interviews, in-person coaching and through two books that I've written on the subject: *The Path to Job Search Success* and *No Medal for Second Place*. Sample chapters of both books can be found on my website: http://www.tompayne.com/job-search-books.html

complex, pressure-cooker sales situations. For example, they helped me overcome the ambush detailed in the first chapter's sales-hell scenario. But I had no idea they were generating a powerful charisma that made me very successful in sales, and in job interviewing as well.

You might wonder, "How can you be certain better nonverbals were behind the success of these jobseekers?"

Prior to working with these jobseekers on their nonverbal behavior I worked with them on their answers to typical questions, how to use stories, and so on. And these verbal elements of charisma, because they used emotion-generating language, helped many to land jobs. But the nonverbally challenged, who were taught these same techniques, remained unemployed.

Then, after I developed a seminar on how to control nonverbal behavior, and began to coach them on this skill set, the continually overlooked jobseekers not only were hired they were passionately pursued. In short, they went from invisible to charismatic in days.

As I stated in the first chapter: Charisma will change the way the world perceives you, and will usher you into a new reality. The world that turned its back on you a week ago will now beat down your door.

As the next chapter shows, gaining mastery over nonverbal behavior turned people (and some hated the idea of selling themselves), into charismatic sales superstars, and they taught me more about the sales process than I ever would have imagined.

4

THE SALES LABORATORY

THE PERFECT SALES LABORATORY

When I volunteered to coach jobseekers in the art of interviewing I never imagined I was stumbling into the perfect sales laboratory. Here was a group of people who, for the most part, had no sales training and yet were required to sell the most complex *product*—themselves—in the most pressure-packed situation—the job interview.

These people were also at a major disadvantage when it came to nonverbal-charisma. Their PEM state was often one of anxiety, and sometimes depression. These feelings produced nonverbal behaviors that expressed nervousness, insecurity and sometimes hopelessness. If their nonverbals were not so obviously bad, I might not have focused on correcting them.

You might think jobseekers would be the most unpromising sales trainees ever, but they all possessed one critical advantage:

> They were extremely motivated to improve their selling skills. Their careers and livelihood depended on it.

Never was this motivation more certain than for a woman I will call Tess.[1] Her amazing story now follows.

---

[1] All of my clients are given fictitious first names.

LIFE IN A CHARISMA-FREE ZONE

Tess is an attractive, engaging sales professional with an English degree from a respected Ivy League school, and a MBA from the University of Chicago. Her resume revealed a track record of high-performance at excellent, respected companies. She was eminently hirable.

So, why had she been out of work for nineteen months? And why had she interviewed with fifty-nine people at twenty-nine different companies, and failed at every opportunity?

I have experienced rejection from a company after interviewing for a job, so I know how that can be an emotionally trying experience. It is likely you've experienced this disappointment as well. I can also imagine how devastating it would be to be rejected by five companies in a row. But it's difficult for me to imagine how empty I would feel after being rejected by twenty-nine companies in a row.

How she avoided falling into a state of learned helplessness is a testimony to her great strength. Tess was a fighter.

A FAILED FIRST ATTEMPT

My first sales laboratory was the Career Transitions Center of Chicago, where I served as a volunteer coach for two afternoons a month.[2] It was there that I first met Tess. As she entered the small office for her coaching appointment, I saw an emotionally-drained person who inspired pity and compassion, instead of confidence.

I said to her, "You seem kind of beat up." She remembered these words and repeated them to me months later. At the time, I did not know how dark her private hell was.

She not only met with me, she also met several other coaches at the CTC. We all tried our best to help her during our coaching sessions, but when she left the CTC she was still unemployed.

Why did we fail?

I believe it is because we equipped her with verbal charisma, but it was being continually undermined by her nonverbals that communicated a different message. She had an inauthentic voice and this verbal-nonverbal

---

[2] When commitments required me to end my volunteer coaching this sales laboratory followed me. Word of mouth about the effectiveness of my job interviewing system spread and job search clients began to seek me out.

disconnect generated a cognitive strain—disbelief—in the hiring authorities she was meeting.

Tess needed to learn how to sell to System 1 by speaking with an authentic voice. Her words could not overcome the nonverbal message she was unconsciously communicating. It said, "I'm nervous, scared, and emotionally exhausted."

We are back at **Charisma Axiom # 4:**

> When our words say one thing
>
> ["I'm talented! I know I can do it! I've got great stories!"],
>
> but our nonverbal behaviors say another
>
> ["I have been drained of the last ounce of confidence that I once possessed."],
>
> people tend to believe our nonverbal voice.

Such was the case for Tess.

WE MEET AGAIN

Several months after she left the CTC I got an email from Tess. It said she wanted me to help her prepare for her next job interview that was one week away. The timing of her contacting me was fortuitous. I developed my system to control nonverbal behavior after she left the CTC. I thought, "This is just what she needs." But I also wondered, "Would it work for her? Is one week enough time?"

We would soon find out, and the results would be unambiguous. Either she would get yet another rejection note, or she'd receive a happy phone call that made her a job offer.

During this week I focused on the techniques in *Part Two* of this book. She passed the first-round of interviews, and then sent me this email. I am copying it just as it appeared, mistakes and all, except for added emphasis and bracketed notes:

> I have good news, I have a second interview scheduled for Monday afternoon with the SVP for [the hiring company] and I am incredibly anxious.
>
> … I think after all of the interviews I've had I am terrified of screwing this up. (and there are around 5 candidates, fyi, but they may have two positions, the recruiter told me). **I"m also**

surprised it's Monday, because she said it might take a while to get on his schedule... [Charisma makes its first appearance.]

> This isn't good nerves. It started as soon as I confirmed the appt for Monday (via phone).

Charisma was exerting its magnetic influence in less than one week. You can see its arrival by the way it produced one of those head-scratching moments that sometimes befuddled my clients. She wrote:

> I"m also surprised it's Monday….

The hiring authorities were responding to Tess's charisma. They wanted to buy what she was selling NOW. She was becoming magnetic, attractive, and able to make them overlook the nineteen-month hole in her resume.

This rushed interviewing process confused Tess, because she was not used to being pursued by these "customers." Instead, she was now used to being overlooked and failing to close the sale. But once she changed the way the world perceived her, she entered a new reality.

The time-strapped Senior Vice President (SVP) sped up the interviewing process for her, because charisma compels people to act in non-rational ways. It defies the rational rules of logic that do not allow for contradictions. For example, you cannot logically say at the same time, "The SVP does not have time to interview you," and, "The SVP has time to interview you." A contradiction is a violation of logic's rules. But charisma's influence puts a different form of logic in play. When a person is affected by it they are subject to the tidal pull of overpowering emotion. There may have been no time for the SVP to interview Tess, but charisma declares, "The SVP will make time to interview you."

CHARISMA'S IMPERMANENCE

Tess had conquered her fears during the first round of interviews, and spoke with a charisma that made them want her. But the second round was coming and, as her email showed, she was terrified of failing for the thirtieth time in a row.

This reveals an important aspect of charisma and this insight becomes **Charisma Axiom # 5:**

> Charisma is not a permanent state. As our PEM state improves or declines, so does our ability to be charismatic.

Even those who possess an overabundance of charisma are not always charismatic. The former U. S. President, Bill Clinton, was a master of nonverbal charisma. But when he angrily shook his finger at the camera, and denied he had had an affair with his intern, Monica Lewinsky, he was not charismatic. His agitated, angry state—expressed perfectly by his nonverbal behaviors—made the charisma that was as natural to him as breathing completely disappear.

When we are physically exhausted, stressed to the point of thinking unclearly, or emotionally upset, we have the attractive power of a refrigerator magnet. In Tess's case, anxiety threatened to overwhelm her just hours before her next round of interviews.

That weekend, prior to her Monday interview on May 4th, she had a hyperventilating, stop-the-car-I've-got-to-get-out, panic attack. I am not a licensed psychologist, so I did not offer medical advice, but I did offer practical advice. I said, "The techniques I've shared with you are designed to create an optimal PEM state. Use them right now. We've got to get this under control and I believe we can." As she noted in follow-up emails that I'll share later, these techniques helped her turn the corner.

ENTER GAME-CHANGING CHARISMA

The May 4th interview went well, and about one week later, after her final round of interviews, I got a call from Tess. It was the voice of someone who had emerged from a joy-deprivation tank. It echoed with ecstasy. She then wrote me the following email that same day, with the emphasis being added by me:

> I got an amazing job offer today from _____, the company that I have been interviewing with. The base is **$20K higher than my last salary**, and the commission is also solid.

> …I am so excited, and wanted to thank you for your help and confidence in me. **I've been out of work for 19 months, and have had 59 interviews in that time.** Perhaps everything is timing... but I have definitely had more confidence the past few weeks.

Tess's job offer shows the impact of charisma. Ask yourself, "When does a hiring company offer someone $20,000 more at the salary line when they've been out of work for nineteen months?"

She would have gladly accepted $20,000 less, and had they merely matched her previous salary she would have jumped for joy. But charisma intervened and ensured she did not have to settle for less.

Tess was and is a salesperson by profession, but for nineteen months she was selling badly and nobody was buying. Then, at the end of this nineteen-month period, she finally closed the sale. This change did not occur because she became smarter (she was already very smart). She did not become more emotionally intelligent, or learn some cool new way to close the sale. Instead, her newfound success was due to her changing the way she was perceived. She then went from being consistently and repeatedly overlooked and rejected, to being attractive and sought after. And note: The only change made between twenty-nine straight failures and success was her developing the ability to control her nonverbal behavior. As the second axiom states:

> **Charisma Axiom # 2:** Charisma is acquired by those who master their nonverbal voice.

I highlight Tess's adversity because it offers this hope: You may feel like you are utterly lacking in charisma, but if you put in the work, then charisma can be yours in days. It may take longer for some, but Tess became charismatic in one week, and she started her journey to charisma at the bottom of a hole she had been digging for nineteen months. Most salespeople are not as emotionally wounded as Tess was, so I believe charisma can be attained by virtually everyone in a few days, not weeks, or months. I've seen it happen in twenty-four hours, as the next story shows.

CHARISMA IN TWENTY-FOUR HOURS

I say a person can become charismatic in one week, but Barbara showed it was possible to become so in one day. When I met her I saw a warm person who was also shy, retiring, and nervous about tomorrow's job interview. She was an unlikely candidate for charisma.

Someone at the CTC suggested she see me and I now had forty minutes of coaching time to help her master her nonverbal voice. So, because of my limited time with her, I focused on just two techniques. When she left she seemed excited about trying them.

After her interview, how long do you think it took before the hiring authority responded to her?

She was interviewing for a job that involved helping people enroll in the Affordable Care Act (aka Obamacare). Since her job was associated with a government program I would assume the response time would be measured in weeks and not days.

I could not have been more wrong. She was called with *a job offer two hours after her interview*. Shy and retiring Barbara became charismatic in less than one day.

Charisma. It compels people to act in ways that are non-rational. Dispassionate, analytical reason would have taken more time to weigh Barbara's merits against the merits of others. But charisma's emotional power intervened and made the hiring authority leap at the chance of hiring her.

CLAUS AND THE DIMENSIONS OF CHARISMA

When I ask jobseekers who are attending one of my seminars, "How many of you feel like you own the room and fill it with your charismatic energy during a job interview?" few hands are raised.

Those who do raise their hands are typically those who radiate strength charisma with little warmth. They feel they are charismatic because they are so self-confident, but they are actually, in most cases, anti-charismatic. Others perceive them as pushy, or arrogant, and this perception repels instead of attracts.

A client of mine, who I will call Claus, suffered from this problem. He was a German national, now living in the U.S., and his nonverbal behaviors communicated all strength and no warmth. He spoke with an intensity that was overpowering. Like a prizefighter during a weigh-in, his eyes would lock yours in a stare down. His tone was loud, startlingly so at times, and forceful. His body looked like a coiled spring. He acted like he might grab a hiring authority by the throat and shout, "Give me the job now!"

Like most of us, Claus was unaware of the impact his nonverbal voice was having. He thought he was simply expressing his extreme degree of self-confidence, and that this was attractive.

All strength and no warmth pushes people away from you, particularly when the person you are meeting is in the driver's seat. Hiring authorities, just like customers, have all of the decision making power on their side. They feel disrespected when their power is not given the deference they feel it deserves. Therefore, anyone who seems to be trying to overpower them is doomed to fail in this contest.

With this we can see how charisma has dimensions, such as strength and warmth. In the next chapter we will see why these dimensions are often out of balance, and revisit Claus's job search journey and the impact of his nonverbal transformation.

5

THE DIMENSIONS OF CHARISMA

STRENGTH AND WARMTH

The two primary dimensions of charisma are strength and warmth. Strength charisma is communicated by a commanding presence. It is focused energy, like a laser beam. It sends the following powerful and attractive message, "I am strong enough to help you achieve your goals."

But when a person's charisma is all strength and no warmth it can repel people, for it is threatening. It suggests, "I have the strength to do great things, and if I have to walk all over you to accomplish this, I will."

When strength is accompanied by warmth it communicates, "I am strong, but I am an ally of yours. I will help you. I am not a threat."

This is important, because System 1, our tireless watchman, is always on duty. It recognizes nonverbal threats instantly, and immediately responds.

All strength and no warmth may, at certain times, be a good thing for a military or a political leader. As Machiavelli wrote in *The Prince*, it is better for the Prince to be feared than loved.

All strength without warmth can generate fear and the late Margaret Thatcher, aka the Iron Lady, used her strength charisma to maximum effect when she was the Prime Minister of the U.K. It was a charisma she consciously cultivated. She even took voice lessons to lower the pitch of her voice to make it sound more authoritative.

The converse, all warmth and no strength, generates love and friendship instead of fear. This might be a useful form of charisma for someone in the hospitality industry, and in other professions. By comparing fear and love, Machiavelli mapped out the primary dimensions of charisma some 500 years ago.

To illustrate the impact of all-strength or all-warmth nonverbals, I will share the experiences of two of my clients, and you've recently met one of them.

A DISORIENTING JOURNEY TO WARMTH

Claus's next interview was with an internationally famous German company that in 2015 generated over $30 billion in revenue. It was a great job for anyone, but for a German national like Claus, it was a prize he desperately wanted to win. Like Tess, he only had a week to prepare for his interview, but this was enough time to gain control of his nonverbal voice.

The company had a few openings in Chicago and they were interviewing a large slate of candidates to fill them. The interviews would take place over the course of an entire week. Claus interviewed on Wednesday, and he hoped to hear some favorable news by Monday at the earliest.

Monday would be a really fast response after an entire week of interviews, but Claus experienced something even more surprising. The next week, when I asked him how it went, he replied:

> I got an offer. But here is what I don't understand. I interviewed on Wednesday and they called me Thursday night to make the offer.
>
> Why didn't they wait until the interviewing was over? They could have called me Friday afternoon if they were in a hurry. Right?
>
> I mean, look, I'm glad they called on Thursday. Don't get me wrong. But it doesn't make sense. They didn't need to. They might have interviewed four superstars on Friday, but one of them wouldn't get an offer because I now occupied that slot.

Claus was struggling to understand what had just happened. He was adjusting to his new reality. One week he was a too-intense jobseeker who made people feel uncomfortable and was quickly eliminated from contention. The next week he was a hotly pursued, top-tier candidate. He felt like he was the same person, but people were treating him like he was someone else. His head was spinning.

I tried to convince him that he had changed. He now had a charisma that he did not have before. I told him:

They rushed to hire you because you became irresistibly attractive to them. You developed the magnetic appeal of charisma that makes people act in non-rational ways.

To call their actions irrational would be harsh and unfair. However, I bet if you asked them for the "reasons" why they rushed to make you an offer they would struggle to put their "reasons" into words.

As Blaise Pascal once wrote, "The heart has reasons which reason knows nothing of." So, the rational, conscious mind struggles to make sense of a decision made by our non-rational, subconscious mind.

Claus would have none of this. He could not believe he had gained the ability to communicate this powerfully in a matter of days. It led him to leap to conclusions that were completely false. For example, he deflected credit away from his performance and gave it to his interviewers. He said:

Look, I have to give the people at [X-company] credit. They went out of their way to make me feel relaxed and comfortable. And so yes, I would agree with you that I needed to be less intense. But in the past, maybe I wasn't as relaxed as I needed to be because I wasn't being interviewed by people who were this professional.

I smiled and said:

You've got it backwards. When you went into the interview projecting confidence, warmth and being comfortable in your own skin, the interviewers felt what you felt. You literally communicated your physical, emotional and mental state to them. They were relaxed and comfortable because you were, and they so enjoyed this interviewing experience that they rushed to hire you. Had you gone in there looking intense, you would have made them feel uncomfortable. People tend not to hire those who make them feel uncomfortable. Instead, they end the interview as quickly as they can.

In working with Claus, I had him focus on balancing his strength charisma with warmth. That's it. This simple tweak to his nonverbal behaviors— adding a smile, a friendly cast to one's eyes, a relaxed demeanor and body language, a gentler, warmer tone of voice, etc.—gave Claus a charisma that was so powerful it befuddled him.

When Claus was all-strength and no warmth he repelled people, and note: He was a salesperson by training and trade. Salespeople often perform poorly in job interviews because the pressure of this sales situation negatively affects their PEM state, and this robs them of whatever degree of nonverbal mastery they may, at other times, possess.

When it comes to expressing an imbalanced form of charisma, salespeople tend to fall in the Claus category. Most salespeople are confident, but some are confident in a way that is perceived as "arrogant." They blindly charge forward as if the purchase order belongs to them and is not a prize to be won by the best salesperson. Their arrogance is off-putting, and not charismatic.

One would think all-warmth charisma would deliver better results, would be less repellent, but it is another path to failure, as Antonia's story shows.

ALL WARMTH AND NO STRENGTH

Unlike the focused laser beam of strength, warmth radiates a diffuse, glowing energy—like a welcoming fire on a winter day—and it is very attractive. When I was coaching Antonia, I observed her expressing a warmth charisma to perfection. It was so natural to her. She looked warm all the time. Her friendly smile, soft eyes, and gentle tone were nonverbal magnets that drew you toward her.

I remember the first time I saw her, how she stood out from a crowd of people. I was giving a seminar and her eyes and smile expressed a gentle encouragement that was overpowering. It was so magnetic that I had to force myself to look away from her. Her warmth made you want to be her friend, because people enjoy basking in the glow of a warm personality. But its lack of authority stopped short of communicating, "I have the ability to take on tough tasks."

Warmth without strength can make you look soft and insubstantial. Antonia was not weak, but she appeared to be. It was a perception that became her reality. This made her journey to charisma the exact opposite of Claus's. He moved away from all strength toward warmth and she moved away from all warmth toward strength.

THE NONVERBAL-VERBAL MISMATCH

Antonia thought she was ready when she interviewed for a coveted position in her field. She was armed with good stories that highlighted her strengths. Her answers to typical questions like, "Tell me about yourself," were honed to perfection. In short, like many a salesperson, she had a successful script, but her nonverbal behaviors undermined her candidacy.

After the interview, she remembered being asked a question about whether or not she was focused on this opportunity. She also remembered her answer. She told the hiring authority, "I think this job is a perfect fit for me. It aligns with my interests and I would be totally focused on it. I'm not looking to do something else."

When Antonia failed to get the job, she asked the hiring authority for helpful feedback and was told, "You seemed unfocused on this opportunity."

This left Antonia confused and very upset. When she recounted this experience to me she began to cry. She asked, "Why did she say this? I told her I was focused on this opportunity! I was very clear on this point."

We are back at

> **Charisma Axiom # 4:** When our words say one thing, but our nonverbal behaviors say another, people tend to believe our nonverbal voice.

In the case of Antonia, her words said, "I am focused like a laser beam on this opportunity." But her warmth charisma, which is gentle and diffuse, said, "I am an unfocused person." And her nonverbal message was what the hiring authority heard and believed.

Salespeople who win some and lose some, and are always finishing in the middle of the pack, are probably guilty of communicating this mixed message. My charisma exercises can correct this uneven performance.

As powerful as charisma is, it will not guarantee you will close every sale. For example, it does not enable you to sell a terrible product that is widely known to be a stinker. Emotions cause the buying decision, and no one wants to be known as the fool that bought the discredited System Z. However, assuming that the product and service playing field is fairly level, charisma can change the trajectory of your sales career, for it does imbue the words you say with a power that speaks to System 1.

ANTONIA DEVELOPS STRENGTH CHARISMA

We met on October 6, 2015, and worked on exercises designed to help her project strength. A few weeks later, on October 21st, she sent me the following email:

> Hi Tom,
>
> I just got out of my interview at _____. I didn't get the job.

Well, that didn't go quite like I had hoped. But the rest of her email illustrates the power of charisma:

> They did decide, however, to meet together with other department heads to start the process of creating a new position that will "better utilize" me.

> They are going to tailor a position to fit my interest in expanding their charitable initiatives and arts education programming. They said they'll be back in touch by Friday to set up another meeting.

Wow! Antonia went from disappointing rejections to, "We want you so badly we are going to design a position that currently doesn't exist, tailor-made for you, so that we can employ you."

Charisma's fingerprints are all over this outcome. She was no longer in the party of the bypassed and overlooked. She switched her party affiliation and now belonged with the sought after and desired. The only thing she did to make this change was she balanced her nonverbal expression by augmenting her warmth charisma with strength charisma.

What I never expected was just how radically charisma would transform Antonia. When I met her after this interview I could see how these charisma exercises literally changed the way she looked. She still expressed warmth, but now her eyes and her facial expression also projected confidence and resolve. Features that once looked warm and soft now looked warm and authoritative. She now held herself differently. Calm, at ease, yet somehow commanding. She looked like a person of substance and the trajectory of her life changed as a result.

Charisma has an enormous impact on sales, because it generates favorable emotions that cause the buying decision. In *Part Three: Verbal Charisma* we will learn how words can also generate these emotions, but words are a slower, more advanced way of communicating thoughts. System 1 is simpler and more primitive in its communication style. It is more visual than verbal, and customers respond immediately and powerfully to nonverbal behavior. They cannot help but do so, because it is how people are programmed to respond.

ATTENTION

Another vital dimension of charisma is attention, or focus. Our attention also needs to be balanced with strength and warmth. Claus's stare-down gaze was focused, but too strong. And Antonia's focus on people was in a dreamy sort of way that seemed unfocused. So, our focus on the other person must be both strong and warm.

Attention-charisma is something everyone should try to develop, because "inattentiveness" is on the rise, and it is a charisma killer. A video that went viral showed a woman walking while texting and then falling into a fountain.[1] To say we are losing our focus in this multitasking age is an understatement.

You've probably experienced this: You are speaking to someone who begins to look at his watch, people passing by, and so on. His inattention communicates the insulting message, "You are unimportant. You are not worth my time and attention."

Inattention has a big emotional impact, because face-to-face talk always involves a relationship. It continually asks, "How am I being treated?" When your System 1 sees how a person is not paying attention to you it comes to the inescapable conclusion, "This person is not treating you well. Therefore, this person is not a friend." And as System 1 sounds the alarm, an uneasy feeling toward this person starts to form in your gut.

However, just as inattentiveness communicates, "You don't matter," warm, focused attention communicates, "You matter a great deal to me. I am your ally and not a threat."

POSITIVE EXPRESSIONS OF LIFE

There is an energy dimension to charisma that is difficult to quantify and define. People with charisma are radiant. They are like fountains of positivity and this energy they express is very attractive. It appeared in the Ambady experiment wherein the subjects identified the following traits— optimism, active, and enthusiastic—by visual, nonverbal behavior alone. It is often seen as a zest for life.

However, we need to be balanced in our expression of this zest for life. People who are too energized—think about someone who looks like they've just had their third triple espresso—can overwhelm the psychological circuit breakers of others. They are so overpowering that they drive people away.

---

[1] The YouTube link is http://bit.ly/2gSXKf8. Her impressive headfirst dive into the fountain, and nonchalant exit, earns her a lot of style points.

In sum, the dimensions of charisma are typically most powerful when they are balanced. They transmit a powerful message that literally alters the customer's emotional state in favorable ways.

THE END OF PART ONE

This concludes *Part One*. I hope it has expanded your understanding of charisma and nonverbal behavior, and that it motivates you to learn and practice the exercises detailed in *Part Two*. The number one reason why the people in my sales laboratory became charismatic is they were motivated to perform the exercises and hopefully secure a job. May your motivation match or exceed theirs. And it should, because the sales profession pays for results, not effort.

If you want to become a top producer, then you must master the most powerful form of communication: Nonverbal communication. Once you do this people will start treating you differently, because charisma will change how you are perceived and usher you into a new reality.

Charisma is the song an optimal PEM state sings with its nonverbal voice. Now it's time to learn how to reprogram System 1, optimize our PEM state, and sing this song.

PART TWO

Charisma in One Week

6

SEE IT, BE IT

THE POWER OF VISUALIZATION

When it comes to acquiring charisma, visualization may be the most important exercise and here is why: It can insert a very specific program into System 1 that can modify and control nonverbal behaviors.

Visualization enabled me to balance my strength charisma with warmth, and generate the charisma that paved the way to my sales success. It also helped me enter the toughest sales situations and prevail.

Before I entered the first chapter's sales-hell scenario, I visualized the challenges I expected to face. I saw the decision maker's anger exploding in my face, and it did. I also saw myself calmly listening to her, and I did. Visualization prevented her insulting behavior from negatively impacting my emotional state, or from provoking me to respond in kind. System 1 was reprogrammed to view her anger not as a threat, but as an opportunity.

It also took away the element of surprise, the very thing that makes ambushes so effective. I was not surprised by her rage because I had seen it in my head many times. Nor was I intimidated by it, because I was always calm, warm and authoritative during my visualization exercises. Visualization is so important to the attainment of charisma it deserves its own axiom:

> **Charisma Axiom # 6:** Visualization is one of the fastest and most effective ways to achieve nonverbal mastery.

There is a reason why I am so strongly encouraging you to embrace this exercise; it is because many of my clients resisted visualizing. It isn't because it is difficult or takes a lot of time. They simply didn't believe it worked. Or they thought it was too New Age for them. That was the stumbling block for the following client of mine, and it prevented him from achieving the charisma he so desperately needed.

PLEASE, DON'T LET THIS BE YOU

He was a CTC client—a white male, about sixty years old—and I had worked with him for over a year. Month after month I would ask him if he was visualizing nonverbal behaviors and each month he would tell me what I could already see, "No, I have not started to visualize just yet."

This might not have been a problem had his nonverbals approached normalcy, but his were so odd that no hiring authority could see past them. He was very smart, creative, and technically gifted, but this powerful mix of talents was invisible. During interviews the only thing the interviewer could see were nonverbals bordering on the bizarre.

His reluctance to practice visualization was sad. Not even the fear of running out of funds was enough to overcome his psychological resistance to this technique. What makes his story even sadder is the way visualization is such a mainstream exercise. Athletes, of all types, swear by it, and the reason it works for them is the same reason it works for mastering nonverbal communication.

THE CASE FOR VISUALIZATION

Just as most people underestimate the impact of nonverbal behavior, they are also unaware of the incredible power of visualization. I could turn to virtually any sport to show you how athletes embrace this exercise, but I've chosen golf because it requires controlling ones thoughts and emotions, along with fine-tuned motor control. A long approach shot over water…water… an endless expanse… a veritable ocean. It is a sport that has seen its top players implode from self-inflicted pressure like this.

How do professional golfers handle this pressure and optimize their PEM state? Many of them turn to visualization. It is widely used today and it was used more than fifty years ago by the greatest golfer of his generation, and perhaps of all time, Jack Nicklaus. In his book, *Golf My Way*, he wrote:

I never hit a shot, even in practice, without having a very sharp, in-focus picture of it in my head. It's like a color movie. First I "see" the ball where I want it to finish, nice and white and sitting up high on the bright green grass. Then the scene quickly changes and I "see" the ball going there: its path, trajectory and shape, even its behavior on landing. Then there's a sort of fade-out, and the next scene shows me making the kind of swing that will turn the previous images into reality. Only at the end of this short, private, Hollywood spectacular do I select a club and step up to the ball.[1]

Jack Nicklaus never hit a shot, even in practice, without visualizing it. As talented as Nicklaus was, he refused to skip this step. It was an essential element in his game. It enhanced his confidence and helped him control the physical behaviors involved in a golf swing. We are also trying to control physical behaviors, and enhance our confidence as well. Visualization checks both of these boxes.

Let's bring this forward to our time. At the moment, Jason Day is one of the top-ranked golfers in the world. The way his performance coach, Jason Goldsmith, describes it, golf is all about getting System 2 to submit to a properly programmed System 1:

The reason why golf is so difficult is because you are starting the action—everything is still, so your intellect [System 2] wants to be involved. Your mind wants to be in control, but the golf swing has to be done on a subconscious level [System 1]. It's impossible to think about the thousands of muscles and tendons and ligaments that have to fire in a perfect sequence in a fraction of a second [System 2's limited bandwidth and speed]. Yet even the best players in the world get stuck in a pattern of trying to consciously make the perfect swing. It doesn't work.[2]

The goal of visualization is to make the golf swing subconscious, automatic, and effortless. That is the goal of visualizing nonverbal behavior as well. In both cases, the number of moving parts exceeds the bandwidth of System 2, but to our visual brains, and our visual System 1, a visualized picture is worth far more than a thousand anxious thoughts and words.

---

[1] Jack Nicklaus, *Golf My Way*, with Ken Bowden, (New York: Simon & Schuster Paperbacks, 2002), p. 79.
[2] Emmett Knowlton, *Jason Day mastered his mental game by adding a 15-step visualization routine before every shot—and now he's the best golfer in the world*, April 6, 2016. Bracketed notes are mine.

FIRST- OR THIRD-PERSON?

When you visualize, do you see the scene unfolding through your eyes, or as a spectator looking upon the scene?

Whether you visualize in the first- or third-person depends on what you are trying to control. Before I give a presentation I am visualizing the scene through my own eyes. I am looking at the audience, connecting with them, watching them smile and nod in response to my presentation.

But I don't stop there. I also visualize this scene as a spectator so that I can visualize my body language as relaxed, fluid, and natural. I see myself comfortably walking around instead of being chained to the podium. I then return to the first-person and see my customers asking questions. They are engaged and interested. And then I move back to the third-person mode and see myself answering questions warmly and encouraging others to join in the interaction.

In visualizing my sales hell scenario I used a third-person view so that I could see the decision maker's fury and my relaxed and calm response. My facial expression was respectful, yet unflinching. My body language was relaxed. I would then see her yelling in my face through my own eyes. I wanted to experience this anticipated ambush in the first person, to make my visualization exercise as real as possible. So choose the viewpoint—first- or third-person—based on what it is you are trying to accomplish.

BUILDING MENTAL MUSCLES

If you are new to visualization, then it might take a few tries before you feel comfortable using this technique, but keep at it, because your comfort level will come quickly. The primary difficulty for most people is staying focused on the visualization exercise for more than a few seconds. This is because the mental muscles required for sustained concentration are atrophied in a large swath of the population.

If this is true for you, don't worry. Atrophied mental and physical muscles can be made stronger. As with physical exercise, you start slow and begin to make incremental progress. Your first visualization exercise may only last one minute, and during this time your mind jumped everywhere. If so, then keep visualizing for one minute every day, a few times a day, until you can finally stay focused the entire time. Then visualize for two minutes the next time and continue to add minutes to your visualization until you reach five minutes.

I never visualized my nonverbal behavior for long periods of time and found that I did not need to. But I would visualize my behaviors often throughout the week preceding an important presentation. A few minutes here, and a few there, was all it took for me, but if you really struggle with your nonverbal behavior, then it may require you to visualize for longer time periods.

TESS AND THE ROAD BACK

I return to the illuminating story of Tess. As you may recall, after she passed her first phone interview she emailed me about how anxious she was about the next round. To help her generate charisma I emailed my reply:

> …Next start visualizing yourself meeting the interviewer, being completely calm and relaxed. You smile and the interviewer smiles back. Mentally/visually answer the "tell me about yourself" question. Do this visualization exercise every day, three times a day. You need to start seeing yourself succeeding, because you are more than good enough to succeed. Hopefully this will get you out of your self-doubting, negative, downward spiral. I wish my words could do it, but even when I tell you the truth about yourself it has a very limited impact. [Tess refused to believe the great things I said about her until I adopted a unique strategy highlighted in the next chapter.] Therefore, focus on visualizing your success to create a new, positive pattern in your brain.

To which she replied, "THANK YOU. Fantastic advice." But the anxiety mounted and erupted in a panic attack during the weekend. When she called me I could tell she was confronting nineteen months of fear. I told her to go for a run and, afterwards, to keep visualizing and engaging in positive self-talk, the subject of the next chapter.

Courageous Tess faced down the demons spawned by living for nineteen months in an emotionally bruising place. She performed these exercises and, though she panicked mere hours before her Monday interview, she was able to reprogram System 1 and regain control of her PEM state. The speed and depth of this transformation testify to the power of aerobic exercise, positive self-talk, and visualization. All three of these subjects will be covered in this part of the book.

FIRST IMPRESSIONS

The most critical moment in sales is the time when your customers first have a chance to see you, and here is what often happens.

We tend to be amped up before a presentation. Butterflies are flying in our stomach. It may take a few minutes before we calm down, our voice begins to sound normal, and we get into a flow. But guess what? Two minutes of nervousness is too long. During that time our customers are automatically, subconsciously assessing us based on our nonverbal behaviors. This assessment takes seconds.

We all know first impressions are powerful, but "why" they are is what makes them either so beneficial or harmful. First impressions are mindsets, and mindsets follow these three rules:

1. They form quickly.
2. They resist change.
3. They incorporate new data to fit the preexisting image.

This explains why it is so tough to change a bad first impression. Once it is set in the customer's subconscious mind—e.g., this person is anxious and lacks confidence—our later display of confidence is either dismissed or reinterpreted to fit the preexisting image.

System 1 is fast, and it is also rigid and non-rational. It sees what it sees, forms its opinion, and its mind is made up. It can be changed, but not easily, so making your best, nonverbal first impression is critical. The way to make sure this happens is to visualize it.

OWNING THE ROOM

I would visualize myself entering a room where customers are seated and others are filing in. Rather than stand behind a podium, anxiously waiting for them to tell me when I could begin, I would see myself roaming around the room introducing myself, smiling, warmly shaking people's hands and telling them, "I appreciate you taking off time from your busy day to attend this presentation. Please feel free to ask questions at any time."

In my mind my body language would be relaxed, and my facial expression and tone of voice would convey a mixture of warmth and strength. I would imagine them smiling in return as I continued to circulate the room and welcome everyone. If I were to choose one word to describe my appearance it would be joy. I would see myself enjoying the moment.

I would also continue to visualize the words I would say to different people. These comments would range from simple small talk, "Hi, how are you? My name is Tom. What's yours?" to humorously asking with a mischievous grin, "Hi, I have a favor to ask you. Is there anyone in this room that I should watch out for? Any troublemakers?"

By doing this I could comfortably walk around the room before any presentation and establish the mindset that I am warm, likable, comfortable in my own skin and very confident. I have yet to say a word about my product, company, or me, but the room is already being sold on all three. And here is the most important outcome: In those critical first seconds when a customer's System 1 is assessing me, I am not nervous in the least. I look like I'm happy to be there, because I am. I am following the program I've visualized and inserted into System 1. As a result, I radiate a confidence that fills the room. I am a beacon of charisma and it is likely my competition is not.

The previous chapter illustrated the strength and warmth dimensions of charisma. Unless you are already very charismatic, it is likely you express one of these dimensions more than the other. Some people are aware of which tendency their nonverbal behaviors express. If you are not sure, then ask a close friend, "Do I appear too strong and lacking in warmth, or too warm and lacking in strength?" Encourage their honesty, because what you project will be obvious to most observers. Then, based on this feedback, begin to visualize yourself expressing the dimension that you are not projecting as effectively as you should.

VISUALIZING STRENGTH

When people fail to radiate strength charisma, visualization is invaluable. The following visualization exercises address this problem:

> Visualize yourself being introduced to a boisterous crowd. The audience keeps chattering away and paying no attention. You then walk up to the podium looking relaxed and confident. You smile at the crowd and make eye contact with several people. Suddenly the audience becomes still and attentive. They sense your authority and they respond to it.

Strong people command attention. In the above visualization exercise, you communicate a quiet strength that does not need to shout or become overly aggressive. We are not trying to visualize strength devoid of warmth. Instead we see ourselves projecting strength accompanied by warmth.

The next exercise is for those who find it difficult to be assertive:

> Visualize entering a large, crowded room and walking through this sea of people to get to the other side. You are standing tall, walking with a confident, energetic stride and as you move forward the sea of people parts. They defer to you. As you pass them you can say, "Good morning," or some other pleasantry, as your strength is balanced by warmth.

Visualization can give you strength-specific nonverbal behaviors. A soft dreamy expression is replaced by a visualized image of a focused facial expression, softened by warm eyes and the occasional smile.

Visualize your body language as being both relaxed, and erect. You stand tall but not rigidly. The gestures made with your hands are natural, and the arm movements flow from your shoulders. Without realizing it, people tend to keep their arms close to their side and gesture with their hands as if their elbows were glued to their rib cage. Their "penguin" arms are a nonverbal expression of fear, or a lack of confidence, and visualization can make this behavior go away.

Just as visualization can help us gain strength nonverbals, they can also give you the warmth behaviors that can make the overly intense, intimidating personality less threatening and far more attractive.

CLAUS AND THE RADIATION OF WARMTH

Remember Claus, the German national who was way too intense? How did he get to the place where he was relaxed and warm? I asked him to prepare for his job interview in the following way:

> Claus, I want you to visualize the following scene. You are walking up to the receptionist and you introduce yourself with a warm smile. You are not in a hurry and you are completely relaxed. So, you make some small talk.

> When you sit down and wait for the interviewer to come and fetch you, you are completely at ease, taking the occasional deep breath while looking around, taking it all in. The deep breaths will help you stay calmer. You see yourself stand up and smile, when the interviewer arrives, and say, "It's so nice to meet you."

> As you walk down the hall to the interviewing room you are making small talk and enjoying it. When asked, "How was the traffic?" You reply, "It could not have been better."

> You are radiating positivity and good will and you can see the interviewer feeling what you feel, smiling in return and enjoying your warmth.

Salespeople are typically not a shy and retiring group of people. Some, unfortunately, are too aggressive in their nonverbal behavior. They are determined to get the sale, and nothing will stop them as they race toward the finish line. Their determination subconsciously becomes an intense facial expression that needs to be warmed up with an occasional smile, and eyes that are more welcoming and less intimidating. Their body language also tends to be a bit too rigid. All of this can be changed by visualizing what Claus visualized.

See yourself walking in to the place where you will be making a sales presentation and introducing yourself to the receptionist. You are radiating warmth and you will continue to express this warmth to every person you meet. As I told Claus, "You do not need to worry about visualizing strength. You have an overabundance of that. So focus on visualizing warmth." The same is true for every salesperson that comes on a bit too strong.

METHOD ACTING

How do actors gain control of their nonverbal behavior? Some of them use techniques developed by Constantin Stanislavski, and later refined by Lee Strassberg. It is often called "method acting." There are many flavors of this technique, and several of them involve visualization.

For example, let's say an actor needs to act sad in a movie scene. He might remember the time he had to attend the funeral of his best friend who died in a car accident. He sees his friend's weeping mother who is burying her young, gifted son. He can feel her as they hug, and can smell her perfume. He is making this memory as sensate as possible. He can see the father looking stoic until the service begins and then sobbing loudly, his whole body shaking. He remembers how incredibly sad this event made him. He relives this moment by visualizing it and it makes him feel very sad. These genuine emotions will then be nonverbally expressed.

Note how I call these visualized emotions "genuine." That is how the body responds to them. Cortisol is a hormone associated with stress and it is elevated in method actors who are performing sad scenes. Visualization actually changes the chemistry of the blood, and as this blood courses through the brain it changes one's emotional state.

SALES AND METHOD ACTING

Here is how a salesperson can use method acting. Recall a time when you achieved an important goal, or were awarded a prize. It was a meaningful accomplishment that made you smile with pride and pleasure. It could be opening a letter that said you were accepted into the university you hoped to enter, or making an impossibly difficult sales plan and being recognized for it. It could be a big sale that you closed. Whatever it is, recall this memory of something that made you joyful.

I've led seminars wherein the attendees recalled three of their proudest achievements and then shared them with the audience. They literally beam with joy and their charisma changes the mood of the entire room. Everyone begins to smile as an individual recounts what he did and why it was so meaningful to him.

During one of these seminars an introverted woman, over sixty years old, went from being someone I might unintentionally overlook to someone I wanted to get to know. As she shared her amazing achievements she grew in depth and dimension. Others felt the same way and sought her out after the meeting to introduce themselves. She was asked to give seminars on the subject of her expertise. She had changed the way the world perceived her and had entered a new reality.

By remembering a joyful time of achievement we recreate this positive emotional state. Just make the scene as visceral as possible. Were there smells associated with this memory? Were there sounds? Did someone shake your hand or pat you on the back? If so, imagine them.

Finally, associate this memory with a phrase. The one I use is, "I did it! And I can do it again and again and again!" I associate this visualization exercise with a phrase so that I can, at a moment's notice, repeat the phrase inside my head and change my mental-emotional state.

This method acting exercise is typically the last visualization exercise I perform before giving a presentation. It is powerful and it is made more so by the self-talk that accompanies it. "I did it! And I can do it again and again and again!"

Now let's move on to the next chapter. Visualization is powerful by itself, but it is made more so by positive self-talk, the exercise that comes next.

7

RERECORDING THE TAPE PLAYING IN YOUR HEAD

CHANGING MY CHARISMA

According to the Mayo Clinic, "Self-talk is the endless stream of unspoken thoughts that run through your head. These *automatic* thoughts can be positive or negative."[1] If this verbal tape playing in our head is negative, or anything but positively reinforcing, then we need to rerecord it.

Self-talk, like visualization, is more powerful than most people imagine. It can also insert a very specific program into System 1 that affects our nonverbal behaviors. I know this to be true because I experienced the way the Army's military self-talk, and the best in brainwashing techniques, reprogrammed me. At Ranger School I was starved, not allowed to sleep for more than a few hours a day, and would sing about killing the enemy during our early morning runs. I still remember the words we shouted during bayonet training:

> Ranger Instructor: What is the spirit of the bayonet?
>
> Ranger Students: To kill!
>
> Ranger Instructor: What two kinds of bayonet fighters are there?
>
> Ranger Students: The quick and the dead!
>
> Ranger Instructor: Which one are you?

---

[1] http://www.mayoclinic.org/healthy-lifestyle/stress-management/in-depth/positive-thinking/art-20043950. My emphasis.

Ranger Students: The quick!

I am not criticizing the U. S. Army's training methods or its goals. It must use them if it is to turn a peaceful civilian into a warrior. But once you pack away your camouflage fatigues, and re-enter the civilian-corporate world, that warrior persona can work against you, and it did against me. I could tell I was far too intense and aggressive in my nonverbal behavior by the way people responded to me. When your assertiveness starts to overwhelm people, you will not succeed in the world of sales.

REWRITING THE SCRIPT

What could I do?

I did what I taught Claus to do. I visualized myself acting warmly toward others. I would see myself smiling, laughing on occasion, and exuding the confidence that tells the world that I am comfortable in my own skin. I then augmented this visualization exercise by repeating the following positive, self-talk script:

> I am a warm person and I radiate warmth that fills the room. It makes me charming and likable.

> I see the value in all people and I treat everyone with kindness and respect, because everyone deserves to be treated this way.

> I am magnetic, charming and enchanting, and I radiate warmth that fills the room.

I was too strong and needed warmth so I began to talk to myself about how I was warm, kind, respectful of others, and so on. Positive self-talk is the perfect complement to visualization. They should be used together. As you visualize the nonverbal behavior you reinforce it with self-talk.

The impact of these two exercises was immediate and dramatic. My warrior strength-charisma was softened and balanced by warmth. People began to respond differently to me. I had entered a new reality, but I did not realize that I had stumbled onto a formula that generated a powerful charisma.

When confronted with the nonverbal problems I saw in jobseekers I thought, "Visualization and self-talk worked for me. Let's see if it works for them." Then, when I saw how the world responded to their charisma, I realized charisma was being generated by their nonverbal behavior change. It was the very same thing that enabled me to sell at a much higher level.

NEGATIVE SELF-TALK

Tess is an example of just how devastating negative self-talk can be. In her head played a tape of self-sabotage that ran night and day. It affected how she thought of herself and poisoned her life. It can have the same impact on any of us, and it affects more people than we would at first imagine.

When I asked Tess if she beat herself up I knew what the answer would be.

"Yes," she said.

"Often?" I asked.

"Probably more often than I should."

At least she was aware of it, and how it was potentially harmful. Most people are either unaware of it, or blind to its negative impact.

I never asked her what kind of self-talk she engaged in, but after nineteen months she was now hypnotized by it. She believed every word she was telling herself. Without realizing it, she was the author of her tragic script that involved bungling every opportunity that came her way.

BREAKING THE SPELL

I was working with Tess when, all of the sudden, without having planned to do this, I began to ask her questions:

> Me: Tess, are you smart?

> Tess: Yes, I think so.

> Me: What makes you think you are smart? Prove it.

> She looked at me strangely. My aggressive stance put her on the defensive and she seemed puzzled by it.

> Tess: Well I went to two of the best universities in the country and I excelled.

> Me: So, you have objective evidence that proves you are smart. This isn't some fantasy of mine, is it? When I tell you, "You are smart and gifted," then I am not trying to flatter you, or make you feel good about something that isn't true. I'm stating an objective fact am I not?

> Tess: Yes.

> Me: Very, very good. Are you likable?

Tess: Yes, I think so.

Me: What makes you think you are likable?

Tess: My customers like me. Several of them became friends of mine and we're still friends. My co-workers like me. I just get along well with a lot of different people.

Me: How about that. You have objective evidence that proves you are likable. Again, we are talking about reality, your reality, and not fantasy. Right?

Tess: Yes.

Me: Are you a hard worker?

This time she smiled. She knew where the game was headed and she liked what it was pointing out. Namely, that she possessed great qualities that a hiring authority would want.

This exercise reveals an important characteristic of effective self-talk. It must be rooted in the reality of one's genuine giftedness or it will not be believed. We are not engaging in an exercise of self-delusion, we are simply affirming our strengths. Everyone is equipped with talents and every talent has great potential value. But for this potential value to be realized we have to first believe we have these strengths, and then remind ourselves that these form the core of our value proposition, and they make us very valuable indeed.

REPETITION

I wrote her the following advice on April 30th and modifications of this could work for any salesperson:

> Start to practice positive self-talking. Tell yourself, "I am a capable, smart, creative, engaging professional who will make any company's team better." Repeat that several times. Come up with your own power statements. We need to reverse the past few years of negative self-talk. You are not stupid, and you are not a loser. Instead tell yourself, "I am stronger as a result of the testing I've been through. My confidence is based on reality, real accomplishments. Temporary situations do not define me. I will do well in this interview because I will perform as I have trained. I look forward to this challenge, because I have mastered this interviewing art."

Her response showed that she was not only engaging in positive self-talk, she was making it her own. She began to repeat the words that resonated within her. Her emailed response reveals the effect it was having on her:

> What I HAVE been doing this week is asking myself "Are you smart?" Yes. "Are you a hard worker?" Yes. "Do people enjoy working with you?" yes. etc. The questions you asked me on Sunday.

> That seems to calm me too. stops the negative talk.

> Thanks again for your confidence... and I'll let you know how it goes!

Her words, "That seems to calm me too. stops the negative talk." show how she was beginning to reprogram System 1. She was starting to tell herself the positive truth and it gave her confidence to face the challenges ahead of her. But more than this, it equipped this struggling salesperson with the charisma to wow the hiring authorities she met in one of the most consequential sales performances of her life. It is unlikely that you will face such pressure during a sales performance, and that makes it much more likely that charisma can be yours in days, if not hours.

When you start performing your visualization and positive self-talk exercises, you will be able to walk into a room full of people and control it. They will not resist your charisma either, for they will find it enjoyable. It will enable you to do things you may have never thought possible as the following story illustrates.

THE MULTI-MILLION $ SALE

Here is an example of the type of visualization-self-talk combination I engaged in before one of the biggest sales I've ever closed. I said to myself:

> When I walk into a room, I own it. [Then I would visualize myself walking into a room and people turning their heads to take note and then gradually gravitating toward me.]

> When I present to my customers they sit riveted, hanging on my every word, nodding their heads, believing what I say. [I visualize myself giving a presentation and the room responding in a way that matches this script.]

> When I am interrupted or heckled I will always respond with kind authority. I will welcome it, thank them for their interruption, and

proceed to win over the room. [I visualize a customer interrupting me, my gracious response, and the rest of the customers smiling in approval.]

That last point, visualizing being heckled and responding warmly to it, proved to be an important part of my preparation.

I was presenting at a large, renowned hospital on the West Coast. The total business for the installed systems was worth over four million $. The competition was intense.

Sitting in the front row, while I presented, was a nurse who kept raising her hand to ask questions she was fed by a competitor. Each time she asked a question I would say, "That's an important question; thank you for asking that," and I would then proceed to answer the implied objection.

I'm not sure she was trying to be annoying, but she was, and not only to me. Everyone in the room was getting tired of her act. Finally, after her fourth question, I stopped the presentation and looked at her, saying nothing. The room was very quiet with all eyes fixed on me. They wondered, "What the heck is he about to do?"

I then asked, "Could you please tell me your name?"

The tension in the room ratcheted up noticeably. Everyone seemed to think I was on the verge of lashing out at her, but that was not my intent.

She squirmed a little in her chair, regained her feistiness and brusquely said, "Doris Johnson."

I then looked up at the audience and said, "I'd just like to say thank you to Doris. She has asked so many good questions covering topics that I might not have covered, but that must be important to you. Otherwise, she wouldn't be asking them. So, thank you Doris. I appreciate it. You've been a great help."

The crowd smiled at the way I artfully turned the tables on their colleague. They knew she was biased against us, and they even knew the company she favored. She'd made that clear on more than one occasion. Doris then sank down into her chair and kept quiet for the rest of the presentation. She did manage to maintain a sour look on her face that probably lasted long after the presentation's conclusion. And yes, without asking for their business, we closed that deal.

RETURNING THE FAVOR

I then decided to return the favor to my competitors who would be presenting after me. Charisma enables you to do these things that might be found objectionable were it not for its enchanting, charming power. It turned out that this over-the-top part of my presentation was probably the final nail in my competition's coffin.

I talked about the stability of our system and the instability of our competitor's systems. Then I took advantage of a shortcoming I knew their system had. The competitive systems took an inordinate amount of time to boot back up once they were shut down. So, I said:

> This is very important. Please note how I am turning off our system. You no longer have an operational nurse call system. It's a life safety system and your patient's lives can depend on it. But notice how quickly our system comes back up. There. It's functioning once again.

> Our competitor's systems can take an embarrassingly long period of time to boot back up. You owe it to yourself to see just how true this is. Please ask them to turn their system off and then reboot it.

Note: I am talking about the competitor and telling the customer important differences between the products. I am also telling them what they should do to evaluate the competitor's product. What nerve! Who was I to think I could exert so much influence over them?

After my presentation I decided to hang around to see my competitor emerge from the presentation room. He did and his boss, in my presence, asked him, "How'd it go in there?"

He smiled and said, "You know. I was dancing." Yes, from one land mine to another.

Next, one of the decision makers came from the room and he motioned me to join him off to the side to speak privately. He said, "We asked your competitor to turn his system off and turn it back on, just like you recommended."

I smiled and said, "How did that work out for him?"

"Not well."

He did not need to follow my request, or tell me what happened in the room, but he wanted to. Charisma has this effect on people. It draws them to you. You become less of a salesperson who is kept at arms length and more of a consultant who is allowed access to the customer's inner circle.

Whatever the sales situation, visualize your mastery of it and augment the power of visualization with positive self-talk. Then, when you enter this scene, the audio-visual tape will begin to play in your head and favorable nonverbal behaviors will follow. It will give you more influence than you can imagine.

FAITH SELF-TALK

Remember Antonia, the woman who possessed powerful warmth charisma, but lacked strength charisma? One of the ways she grew powerfully in this strength dimension was by engaging in self-talk that leveraged her faith. It is one of the most powerful forms of self-talk because it is based on core beliefs and, as previously stated, our positive self-talk must be based on things we actually believe to be true.

During a coaching session I had the following conversation with Antonia:

> Me: Do you mind if I ask you, "What is your faith?"

> Antonia: Jesus.

> Me: [I smiled at that unique way of answering my question and said...] Okay. You are a Christian. Now I'm going to ask if you believe certain things about the Christian faith. Okay?

> Antonia: Sure. Go ahead.

> Me: Do you believe you are a child of God?

> Antonia: Yes.

> Me: Do you believe you are indwelt by the Spirit of God, and that God lives in you?

> Antonia: Yes.

> Me: Do you believe that God loves you?

> Antonia: Yes.

> Me: I want you to start engaging in the following positive self-talk because it is based on your core beliefs. Few things can be more real or more powerful for you. Start saying to yourself, "I am a child of God, filled with the Spirit of God. I have nothing to fear, because God loves me. His almighty Spirit dwells in me and gives

me the strength to accomplish all that He intends for me to accomplish." Can you comfortably say this?

Antonia: Yes. I believe it.

She then engaged in this faith-based, positive self-talk to help her grow in the strength dimension of charisma.

You may recall that in her previously quoted email, she wrote about a company creating a position for her. I cut that email short but will now show the rest of it.

> They said they'll be back in touch by Friday to set up another meeting.
>
> I can't thank you enough—I was in the bathroom ... repeating what you said to me: I am a child of God, endowed with the Holy Spirit. My God is my strength.
>
> All my thanks,
>
> Antonia

Antonia went from being perceived as a warm, likable, insubstantial person, to being someone people sought to have on their team. She changed how she was perceived by modifying her nonverbal behaviors. Instead of being rejected for opportunities companies began to create them for her.

FAITH-BASED WARMTH

If you are a person of faith, and you need to project more warmth, then visualize yourself being warm toward others and combine it with faith self-talk. You might use words like, "God is love and I am to love my neighbor as myself. I delight in expressing this love by being warm, hospitable and accepting toward everyone I meet."

It does not matter what your faith is when it comes to using this technique. What matters is this, "Do you firmly believe what your faith holds to be true?" As I tell clients:

> If you believe in Jesus and the Holy Bible, or in Mohammed and the teachings of the Quran, or in worshipping oak trees, that is between you and your God. I am not here to change that. However, if your faith is emotionally meaningful and significant to you, then why not leverage it in your positive self-talk? Positive self-talk is about affirming the good that you believe to be true about yourself.

It requires belief, or faith. So leverage that which you believe most deeply.

POSITIVE SELF-TALK AND POSITIVE THINKING

According to the Mayo Clinic, positive self-talk leads to positive thinking and this impressive list of benefits:

> If the thoughts that run through your head are mostly negative, your outlook on life is more likely pessimistic. If your thoughts are mostly positive, you're likely an optimist — someone who practices positive thinking.
>
> **The health benefits of positive thinking**
>
> Researchers continue to explore the effects of positive thinking and optimism on health. Health benefits that positive thinking may provide include:
>
> - Increased life span
> - Lower rates of depression
> - Lower levels of distress
> - Greater resistance to the common cold
> - Better psychological and physical well-being
> - Reduced risk of death from cardiovascular disease
> - Better coping skills during hardships and times of stress [2]

Positive thinking flows from a positive mental attitude, and note how it optimizes our PEM state. It generates lower levels of distress and depression and improves our psychological and physical well-being. This produces charismatic nonverbals. Therefore, one of the primary goals of combining visualization with positive self-talk is to create those attitudes that generate charisma, and so much more.

Changing your attitudes can change your life. This may sound way over the top, but attitudes have such sway over our lives that they literally can hold the power of life and death as the next chapter will show.

---

[2] op cit., www.mayoclinic.org.

8

CHANGE THE ATTITUDES, CHANGE THE PERSON

ATTITUDE IS EVERYTHING

Attitudes are orientations of the mind, or dispositions that guide our thoughts and feelings. The possessor of a "cheerful" attitude feels cheerful much of the time, and this feeling, like all feelings, is nonverbally expressed. Looking cheerful is a part of being cheerful, just as looking surly is a part of being surly.

Note how attitudes—like cheerfulness and surliness—are inextricably linked with emotion and nonverbal expression. The same is true for the attitudes that are essential to charisma:

- Confidence is a feeling of self-assurance and self-belief. It is an attitude, because it disposes the mind to think, "I am more than able to handle this situation or task." Charismatic people feel confident and, therefore, look confident.

- Kindness is a warm, friendly orientation toward others. It is a feeling that appreciates and values others. Charismatic people tend to express warmth.

- Positivity is a feeling of optimism, an orientation of the mind toward solutions rather than problems. It is upbeat and radiant.

It is impossible to separate our attitudes from the emotions we feel and express. Once favorable attitudes take root they make our nonverbal charisma more enduring and organic. This alone would make attitudes a force to be reckoned with, but they have a soul-deep connection with our life that makes them even more powerful than we might imagine.

THE POWER OF LIFE AND DEATH

Two stories follow, one from a tragic time in history and the other from the everyday life of a salesperson. Both situations were challenging, but few stories could be more challenging than this.

Viktor Frankl's was a Jewish neurologist and psychiatrist in Austria during the 1938 unification of Austria with Nazi Germany. From that time on he saw all of his freedoms and privileges stripped away. In 1938 he could no longer treat "Aryan" patients. In 1940 he started work at the only hospital open to Jewish doctors. In 1942 he was sent to the Theresienstadt concentration camp as a common laborer. He then worked in the camps until their liberation in 1945.

Remarkably, he did not leave the camps a broken man. What saved him was his attitude toward his situation. He wrote:

> We who lived in concentration camps can remember the men who walked through the huts comforting others, giving away their last piece of bread. They may have been few in number, but they offer sufficient proof that everything can be taken from a man but one thing: *the last of human freedoms—to choose one's attitude to a given set of circumstances*, to choose one's own way.[1]

For me, the most important part of this story is the way Frankl took responsibility for the attitude he had even while living in the worst of circumstances. He did not blame the Nazis for his attitude, though we certainly would excuse him if he did. Instead, he accepted that his attitude toward his circumstances was a freedom that the Nazis could not take from him.

Frankl understood the power and importance of attitudes, and that in the camps a hopeful attitude was a matter of life and death. In his book, *The Search for Meaning*, Frankl wrote that those with hopeful attitudes, who looked to a better future, had a chance to survive. But once someone lost hope they would die, sometimes within hours.

---

[1] Viktor E. Frankl, *The Search for Meaning* (Boston: Beacon Press, 1959), pp. 65-66. Emphasis mine.

Attitudes wield great power over our lives and we are responsible for them, regardless what the circumstances may be. This had a particularly important impact on a salesperson who came to me for help.

THE FALL FROM POSITIVITY

Carla typically radiated positive energy. But that was before she experienced the hyper-critical culture that came with her new job. The company's founder and CEO was the source of this attitude and it infected the entire organization. It took a while, but it eventually infected Carla, and she became a miserable shell of herself.

One day I got a call from Carla. She asked me to help her master her sales presentation, because her managers, from the CEO on down, told her that they didn't like her pitch to her customers. She told me, "They say it sounds canned. They think I lack confidence. And they hate the way I nervously fidget while speaking to customers."

Then she added this sharp-edged critique, "And my CEO is a bully who plays mind games with people."

The negativity toward her job came pouring out. It was so forcefully stated that I wondered if she was overstating things. So, I asked her to give me an example of a mind game the CEO, who I will call Greg, had played on her.

"How about this one," she replied. "I was just hired and Greg goes with me on a presentation. He told me, 'Don't worry. I'll handle the presentation.' I was glad, because I was still new to the job and had not had time to master it. Then he starts the presentation by saying, 'I'd like to introduce Carla who will now give the presentation.' He blindsided me when I was totally unprepared. Who treats people like this?"

"Psychopaths?" I wondered out loud. "Prison is where the dumb ones end up, while the smart ones become CEOs."

That probably sounded right to Carla who was stuck, for the moment, in a bad place. She now had a negative attitude about her work and, unfortunately, attitudes express themselves. She went from being a dynamic, successful salesperson to a nonverbal train wreck who was failing to sell much of anything.

When I did a brief role-playing exercise with her, where I was the customer and she was making her pitch to me, it was passionless. There was no conviction in her voice. I can imagine that as her customers listened to her, their System 1 was shouting, "She doesn't believe what she is saying so why should you!"

Her environment had succeeded in beating her down and the loss of her positive attitude was collateral damage. She was now anxious and fearful, and for good reason. She believed, quite rightly, that she was living on borrowed time at work.

"Carla," her boss said, "I'd like to see updated files on all of your customers." That alone signaled an imminent termination. But what made her feel even more anxious was a scheduled visit from Greg, the CEO. All of the sudden, he wanted to work with her for three days.

She assumed he scheduled this call so that he could tell her she was fired.

THE POWER OF POSITIVITY

The downsides of this situation are pretty obvious, but do you see the positives? This is an important question, because a positive attitude looks for the positives in any situation, and also looks for ways to leverage them. It is not some Pollyannaish attempt to deny the negative in this or any other situation. Instead, it operates according to this understanding: Looking only at the negative is paralyzing. It makes the negative look bigger and more powerful than it actually is, and this keeps us from acting to influence this situation however we can.

Carla's nonverbal behavior formed a mindset within management that she was a bad hire. She fidgeted in front of customers and played with her hair, nonverbal signals of nervousness, not confidence. Three days with Greg gave her the opportunity to start changing management's negative mindset. This would not be an easy task because mindsets are stubborn. Once set in place they do not gently leave the scene, but three days might get Greg to perceive her differently. Once we looked at Greg's visit in a positive light, it became an opportunity for something good to happen.

Additionally, Carla could change the passive role she was playing. She was like a piece of steel that was only taken out of the blast furnace so that it could be beaten by a hammer. She was being reshaped by others and was allowing it. This needed to change. She needed to become a positive force that shaped her situation. In other words, she needed to become the hammer and deliver her own blows by controlling what she could. And that is what she did.

HER PATH TO A NEW ATTITUDE AND A NEW LOOK

Just as visualization and self-talk can create a positive attitude it can also help recover one that was lost. So, I had her visualize her upcoming meeting with Greg, walking confidently up to him, warmly shaking his hand, looking him directly in the eye and telling him how she looked forward to working with him. (Positivity in action!)

I asked her to visualize him interrupting her, as he frequently did, and her calmly accepting the interruption, smiling confidently, and not being flustered by it at all. (It's all good!)

She needed to see him being hyper-critical, and her listening attentively, not showing either timidity or anger. And then, when he was finished, thanking him for the critique and letting him know she appreciated his candor, valued his opinion and would start to work on these issues immediately. (Always positive, always!)

I also told her to engage in positive self-talk, because it works so well with visualization. As she visualized her positive, confident nonverbal behaviors I told her to say things like: .

> I am a strong, successful salesperson and I radiate confidence.
>
> Whatever Greg's impression of me, it is about to change for the good. He will now see me in the best possible light.
>
> I am clothed in charisma. I am influential and unstoppable.
>
> I am going to enjoy this time with Greg. However he acts, my confidence and poise will not be shaken.[2]

In short, I was preparing her for challenges that she could anticipate facing, just as I had prepared for the raging decision maker in the first chapter.

After these exercises, the only question I had was, "Would she be a hammer or remain the iron ingot that was only taken from the fire to be beaten up?"

CHANGING THE WAY YOU ARE PERCEIVED

Greg was knocked off balance when he met the new Carla. His first words indicated his confusion, and the positive impression she was making, "Have you done something with your hair? Is this a new outfit?"

She smiled and said, "A little bit of both."

He said, "Whatever you've done. It looks good on you."

Something was different. System 1 saw it and was alerting Greg to this change, but he could not put his finger on what it was. He was stuck at card

---

[2] These positive self-talk suggestions are copied from an email I sent to Carla.

fifty. He had a gut feeling that something about her was different but he could not articulate it.

His existing mindset of "Carla the underachiever" was being modified and the rest of his visit went from dread-inspiring to largely positive and productive. But the most important change it produced was this: Carla could now see how the charisma exercises I once taught her for job interviews needed to be a part of her daily sales life. She experienced how her attitudes impacted her charisma and changed her relationship with her management, her customers and herself.

Carla was fired about three weeks after her meeting with Greg. His mind was made up and charisma could only produce a temporary stay of execution. But everything turned out fine. Within three weeks she was able to secure a new job with a company possessing a humane culture, and she is now performing at a much higher level.

HOW DO YOU SEE YOURSELF?

One of the most powerful influences on our PEM state is how we think and feel about ourselves:

> While it is of course also true that your performance shapes your self-concept, the feedback loop goes both ways: *Your self-concept shapes your performance.* You can improve your performance by changing your core beliefs.[3]

How do you view yourself? What is your self-image, or your attitude about yourself? If you do not have a healthy self-image, then what can be done about it?

The first step is self-acceptance, and this sounds so easy, but self-rejection is far more common than you might think. It occurs in countless ways. One form of self-rejection is to envy the giftedness of others and minimize the value of one's own gifts.

I was training a European sales team and one of the modules was designed to acquaint them with their strengths and then leverage them during their selling activities. Toward that end, they all took the StrengthsFinder assessment.

---

[3] David Feinstein, Donna Eden, Gary Craig, *The Promise of Energy Psychology: Revolutionary Tools for Dramatic Personal Change* (New York: Penguin Group (USA) Inc., 2005), p. 132.

One of the salespeople said, "I'm having a tough time accepting the results. I thought I would have scored much higher in some of the strategic thinking strengths."

He did not have a single strategic thinking talent in his top five strengths. Where he had scored highly were in the relationship-building strengths. Three of his top five strengths were empathy, harmony and positivity, and he wasn't happy about it. He thought they were weak.

He was naturally charismatic and unaware that this great strength of his elevated his selling capabilities to an elite level. His "weak" strengths enabled him to read people, adapt to the situation, exude warmth and positivity, captivate and attract. Yet here he was, speaking disparagingly about his great strengths.

I replied, "Are you kidding me? These strengths are what separates you from your peers. You have off-the-chart people skills. This is highly charismatic. It is why people are drawn to you."

Whatever you do, cherish your gifts. They are your unique value proposition. They make you, you.

We will revisit this idea of self-acceptance again in the chapter entitled *The Power of Being Present*. But now it is time to move on and look at the attitude we have toward others.

PEOPLE OR OBJECTS?

What is your attitude toward other people? Your actions will often reveal this more clearly than your thoughts. For example, do you treat people as if they are objects, things lacking in value, or as people who have intrinsic worth?

The following story illustrates how our attitude toward others affects the way we act. The fictional character who is speaking is named Bud:

> About a year ago, I flew from Dallas to Phoenix on a flight that had open seating. While boarding, I overheard the boarding agent say that the plane was not sold out but that there would be very few unused seats. I felt lucky and relieved to find a window seat open with a vacant seat beside it about a third of the way back on the plane. Passengers still in need of seats continued streaming down the aisle, their eyes scanning and evaluating the desirability of their dwindling seating options. I set my briefcase on the vacant middle seat, took out the day's paper, and started to read. I remember peering over the top corner of the paper at the people

> who were coming down the aisle. At the sight of body language
> that said my briefcase's seat was being considered, I spread the
> paper wider, making the seat look as undesirable as possible.[4]

In the first part of this story, Bud, who was on a mission to keep the seat
next to him vacant, was viewing the people coming on board as potential
nuisances, threats to his space, etc. They weren't people with an equal right
to this open seat; they were "objects."

His nonverbal behavior communicated, "I don't want you near me. Move
on!" This attitude that objectifies people not only affected how he thought
and felt about others, it affected how he acted toward them. He wanted to
be repellent and his nonverbal behaviors achieved this.

Next, Bud contrasted his territorial performance to another airplane
experience.

> About six months ago, Nancy and I took a trip to Florida.
> Somehow there was a mistake in the ticketing process, and we
> weren't seated together. The flight was mostly full, and the flight
> attendant was having a difficult time trying to find a way to seat us
> together. As we stood in the aisle trying to figure out a solution, a
> woman, holding a hastily folded newspaper came up behind us,
> from the rear of the plane, and said, "Excuse me—if you need two
> seats together, I believe the seat next to me is vacant. I'd be happy
> to sit in one of your seats."[5]

In this story the woman saw Bud and his wife as people, not objects, and as
a result her warmth and kindness found an opportunity to express itself.

When we start to adopt an attitude that everyone has value and no one
should be treated like an object, we begin to express warmth to all people.
As our feeling toward others changes, so do our nonverbal behaviors and
our actions, and our charisma quotient improves.

The bottom line: Our attitude toward ourselves, and others, generates
feelings that affect our nonverbal behaviors and, therefore, our charisma.

SUMMARY

Nonverbal behaviors produce, in the minds of others, automatic,
subconscious assessments that become mindsets. These mindsets shape

---

[4] The Arbinger Institute, *Leadership and Self-Deception: Getting Out of the Box*
(San Francisco: Berret-Koehler Publishers, Inc., 2010), p. 32
[5] The Arbinger Institute, p. 33.

how people perceive us. We can be seen as confident, capable, warm, likable, and believable, or incapable, unsure, unlikable and hard to believe. A salesperson's success or failure often depends on how they are perceived.

Visualization and positive self-talk not only reprogram System 1, inserting specific nonverbal programs into it, they can also change how we think and feel. These two exercises, by themselves, can generate charisma. But the next exercise is perhaps the most effective way of optimizing our PEM state.

9

THE GOLDEN KEY

THE CONFIDENT CLIENT

Erin attended one of my seminars on mastering nonverbal communication and, after it was over, she confidently walked up to me and said, "I could attend the seminars and workshops of the Career Transitions Center, but I don't want to take that much time. I want to work directly with you and speed up this process. I am confident I can find a new opportunity quickly. Will you send me a coaching proposal?"

She was the face of confidence and strength charisma, without being too pushy.

I said, "Sure," got her contact information, gave her my card and soon we were working together.

THE GOLDEN KEY TRANSFORMS

We've seen how charisma is not a permanent state. We've just seen how a positive attitude can be crushed and replaced by negativity. Confidence is another attitude that we can lose. For when our situation changes, and we are confronted by a task that we know we are unprepared to take on, our feelings of insecurity can mount and produce a crippling level of anxiety and stress. Bye-bye confidence and adios charisma.

I saw this erosion of confidence in Erin. Part of her coaching package involved being videotaped during a mock interview. Replaying this video showed the client the communicative power of their nonverbal voice. Until people see how their nonverbal behaviors are betraying them they are less motivated to work on fixing this issue.

Many people are nervous before role-playing exercises like mock interviews, but they are able to relax and perform well after five minutes or so. Not Erin. Her performance was poor from start to finish. She looked stiff, almost robotic on tape. Her attempts at humor fell flat. While we were reviewing the tape, I stopped before finishing and said, "I'd like to do this again in a day or two."

When she came to the second session she seemed more relaxed and comfortable in her skin. We sat down and conducted the interview, and while reviewing the tape we could both see the dramatic improvement over the last session. It was like I had videotaped a different person.

When I asked Erin what she did to perform so much better for the second mock interview, she replied, "I ran this morning."

Aerobic exercise is like a golden key opening the door to physical, emotional and mental health. I think you will find its ability to impact your PEM state favorably to be nothing short of amazing. And since nonverbal behavior is an expression of our PEM state, this makes aerobic exercise one of charisma's best friends.

However, if you are not currently exercising aerobically, be careful. If it is pursued too aggressively by someone who is out of shape, then the results can be fatal. There is a reason why there are defibrillators in offices where they conduct stress tests of the heart.

That said, virtually everyone can gradually work their way up to aerobically exercising. If you are in the "out-of-shape," or "rarely exercise" category, then start with walking. Slowly build up the pace and distance of your walking while monitoring your heart rate and paying attention to what your body is telling you. When walking is no longer a strain, progress to jogging and walking, and then to jogging.

When ready, up the intensity to jogging and running, and then just running. But if your heart rate gets too elevated, then stop running or jogging and walk slowly until it enters a safe range. Your maximum heart rate (MHR) is 220 beats per minute (BPM) minus your age. So, if you are a forty-year old, your MHR is 180 BPM (220 -40 = 180). You should keep your heart rate safely below this. For example, 90% of your MHR (for the forty-year old it is 162 BPM) would be a good ceiling for the aerobically healthy to stay under.

EMOTIONAL OPTIMIZATION

Neurotransmitters are chemicals that brain cells, or neurons, release to enable the transmission of an impulse from one neuron to another. They enable neurons to communicate, and each neurotransmitter has different functions. The three we will concentrate on are serotonin, dopamine and norepinephrine, because these are the ones targeted by most mental health drugs:

> Prozac, the anti-anxiety and anti-depression drug, targets serotonin. Serotonin influences mood, impulsivity and acts like the policeman of the brain, because it helps control brain activity.

> Dopamine is the neurotransmitter targeted by the drug Ritalin that is prescribed to treat attention-deficit/hyperactivity disorder, or ADHD. Dopamine is involved with reward, learning and attention.

> Norepinephrine affects our motivation level and attention, among other things.

Due to their impact on a wide spectrum of emotional and mental states, our neurotransmitters must be kept in balance. Aerobic exercise does this:

> …I tell people that going for a run is like taking a little bit of Prozac and a little bit of Ritalin because, like the drugs, exercise elevates these neurotransmitters. It's a handy metaphor to get the point across, but the deeper explanation is that *exercise balances neurotransmitters —along with the rest of the neurochemicals in the brain.* And as you'll see, keeping your brain in balance can change your life.[1]

ANXIETY

Erin was a nervous wreck as she was preparing for job interviews, but aerobic exercise calmed her anxiety and transformed her nonverbal behaviors. It had this impact because…

> …the majority of studies show that aerobic exercise significantly alleviates symptoms of any anxiety disorder. But exercise also helps the average person reduce normal feelings of anxiousness.[2]

---

[1] John J. Ratey, MD, Eric Hagerman, *Spark: The Revolutionary New Science of Exercise and the Brain* (New York: Little, Brown and Company, 2008), p. 37. My emphasis. [I highly recommend this well-written, interesting book.]
[2] Ratey, Hagerman, p. 92.

In 1997 Dr. Andreas Broocks conducted a randomized, placebo-controlled trial on agoraphobics. This phobia makes people perceive the environment to be unsafe. It can make them fear crowded and enclosed spaces where they might feel trapped, and open spaces as well.

Broocks's experiment divided his subjects into three groups: one that exercised, one that was treated with drugs, and one that was given a placebo. The exercise group did not start producing positive results, equal to the drug group, until the tenth week. The delay was caused by the subjects inability to run outside until week six, because of their fear of open spaces.

What about panic attack levels of anxiety that Tess experienced?

Prior to her Monday interview, the one giving her a bad case of nerves, I offered Tess the following advice:

> You are funny. You are worried about your competitors and they should be worried about you. Yes, go for some intense aerobic activity right now, and also do this before the face-to-face interview. Your afternoon schedule should make this easy to do.

A good amount of research indicates aerobic exercise is a great way to reduce anxiety, and if it worked for her—and it did—it can work for you.

Salespeople are often placed in pressure cooker situations. This can lead to a stumbling, uncomfortable performance in the crucial first few minutes. A way to combat this is aerobic exercise a few hours before the presentation. It will calm your anxiousness and improve your ability to think. The bottom line is this: Aerobic exercise is good for the health of the body, and it helps us achieve an optimal emotional state.

DEPRESSION

The connection between exercise and treating depression is a strong one.

> In fact, it is largely through depression research that we know as much as we do about what exercise does for the brain. It counteracts depression at almost every level.

> In Britain, doctors now use exercise as a first-line treatment for depression....[3]

Many salespeople reading this may be thinking, "I've never been depressed, or prone to feelings of anxiety." And if you can truthfully say

---

[3] Ratey, Hagerman, p. 114.

this, then I am sincerely happy for you. However, it is highly likely there is stress in your life, and exercise will help you deal with it. This is important because stress is the great disabler. Our brains don't work well when we are under stress.

WHEN SYSTEM 2 GOES DARK

The stress response is an amazing thing. It is doubtful we would have ever survived as a species without it. It redirects all of our body's energy to where it is needed to fight, fly or freeze.

Imagine you are hunting on the savannah and a lion appears. Without seeking your conscious permission, System 1 will take over and set in motion a physiological cascade of changes designed to keep you alive. The heart starts pumping harder, the bronchial tubes in the lungs dilate, adrenaline and cortisol are released into the bloodstream, along with glucose stores to give you the energy to fight this beast or run like mad.

Certain processes that require the body's energy are shut down, because they aren't needed at this moment. Digestions stops, and since you don't need to reason abstractly, the prefrontal cortex, the seat of your higher mental processes, goes dark. You are now operating on a more instinctual level. And all of these changes are automatic and outside of your control.

This is great when faced by a man-eating lion, but the stress response is not discriminating. Virtually the same response is activated by the common stresses of daily life, for example, when giving a presentation, which is a form of public speaking:

> If you've ever faced a nerve wracking public-speaking situation, you've experienced this shift in the form of a racing heart and cotton mouth. *Your muscles and your brain get stiff, and you lose all hope of being flexible and engaging.* [Bye-bye charisma—my note] …None of this is particularly helpful when you're up at the podium, but the body responds in essentially the same way whether you're staring down a hungry lion or a restless audience.[4]

The stress response affects our ability to think because the prefrontal cortex is acutely sensitive to stress.

> The pre-frontal cortex (PFC)—the most evolved brain region— subserves our highest-order cognitive abilities. However, it is also the brain region that is the most sensitive to the detrimental affects

---

[4] Ratey, Hagerman, p. 64. My emphasis.

of stress exposure. Even quite mild acute uncontrollable stress can cause a rapid and dramatic loss of pre-frontal cognitive abilities.[5]

EXERCISE AND STRESS

To be charismatic we need to keep our stress level under control and exercise helps us do so. Dr. Robert Sapolsky, a professor of biology, neuroscience, and neurosurgery at Stanford University, wrote the following about exercise and stress reduction:

> Exercise is a great counter to stress for a number of reasons.
>
> ...[E]xercise makes you feel good. ...And most of all, the stress-response is about preparing your body for a sudden explosion of muscular activity. You reduce tension if you actually turn on the stress-response for that purpose instead of merely stewing in the middle of some time-wasting meeting.
>
> Finally, there's some evidence that exercise makes for a smaller stress-response to various psychological stressors.[6]

Aerobic exercise combats stress and helps us function at a higher cognitive level than a stressed-out version of ourselves. If you are preparing for an important sales presentation, or a high-level meeting with executives who are considering your offering, then exercising before the event is highly recommended.

Aerobic exercise does not just counter stress, anxiety and depression, it actually helps our brains to function better.

IMPROVED BRAIN FUNCTION

Exercise can enhance our cognitive powers after just one workout. In the following experiment adults, aged fifty to sixty-four, were split into two groups. One group ran for thirty-five-minutes on a treadmill and elevated their heart-rate to between sixty and seventy percent of its maximum. The other group watched a movie. Both groups were cognitively tested before exercising or watching the movie, immediately after, and twenty minutes later.

In the "no surprise" category, the group that watched a movie showed no improvement in cognitive performance.

---

[5] Amy F. T. Arnsten, "Stress Signaling pathways that impair prefrontal cortex structure and function: Nat. Rev. Neurosci. 2009 Jun: 10(6): 410-422.

[6] Sapolsky, p. 401.

…but the runners improved their processing speed and cognitive flexibility after just one workout. Cognitive flexibility is an important executive function that reflects our ability to shift thinking and to produce a steady flow of creative thoughts and answers as opposed to a regurgitation of the usual responses. The trait correlates with high-performance in intellectually demanding jobs. So if you have an important brainstorming session scheduled, going for a short intense run during lunchtime is a smart idea.[7]

Exercise also "prepares and encourages nerve cells to bind to one another, which is the cellular basis for logging in new information…."[8] I highly recommend exercising before rehearsing for a presentation, or tackling a difficult problem.

CONCLUSION

Visualization, positive self-talk and aerobic exercise are the three exercises I taught the members of my sales laboratory. And, in my consulting capacity, I've taught it to sales forces as well. These three exercises generate charisma and positive attitudes.

So, why not stop there? Why add two more exercises?

Because some people have difficulty being present, or in-the-moment, and this inability to focus on their customer is weakening their charisma, if not entirely destroying it. The best way to develop this focus charisma is through mental exercises like concentration and mindfulness meditation.

If you have no issue with focusing on your customers, and no interest in learning about meditation, then you can skip these two chapters. But meditation offers benefits that exceed being able to stay focused for longer periods of time. It helps people handle the stress of life, and sales certainly can offer many stressors throughout the day. The ability of meditation to reduce stress is backed by hundreds of research studies.

Finally, I am convinced that concentration meditation, the subject of the next chapter, cannot only generate charisma by itself, it can also generate creative insights into how you can grow your business.

---

[7] Ratey, Hagerman, p. 54.
[8] Ratey, Hagerman, p. 53.

10

THE LASER-FOCUS OF CHARISMA

MENTAL EXERCISE

Meditation changed my life.

When I was a little kid I was unable to focus my attention. I loved to daydream and let my mind wander far and wide. But after I began meditating my "monkey mind" that jumped everywhere was put on a tight leash.

I got to the point where I could easily meditate for an hour and the effect it had on my grades was astonishing. I went from Cs and Ds to As.

As my mind started to function at a much higher level I grew in confidence. I happily accepted difficult challenges—no, I sought them—because I knew they weren't bigger than me. "I can do it," became a core belief. Gaining control of your mind, and having it function at a much higher level, is a great confidence booster.

As this confidence grew it became readily apparent to others. When I went overseas to study psychology at St. Andrew's University in Scotland, several people commented on how I had charisma. I did not solicit these comments, nor was I trying to draw attention to myself. Charisma's power of attraction was automatically and effortlessly doing this for me.

Based on my experience, I believe concentration meditation is an exercise that can generate charisma by itself. And if you aerobically exercise, it can be easily integrated into your everyday routine without adding a minute to your time schedule. It will also change your perception of the time it takes to complete your aerobic exercise. The time will fly by. You will learn how this all comes together in the chapter entitled *The Charisma Exercise Schedule.*

"HOW AM I BEING TREATED?"

Let me briefly summarize what I've covered previously. What makes the attention we pay to another person so powerful is this rule of communication: *Face-to-face talk is always about a relationship and the way we are being treated.* It cannot be otherwise, because System 1 is hardwired to fulfill its role of a watchman. It is always on and monitoring the horizon for threats, because a person who is friendly one minute can become threatening the next.

A social practice that offends System 1's sensibilities is inattention. When someone fails to pay attention to us, he communicates, "You don't matter. You don't deserve my attention."

On the other hand, giving someone our undivided attention is extremely attractive and charismatic. It is the heart of focus charisma, and courtship behaviors show just how powerful this form of charisma can be.

COURTSHIP BEHAVIORS AND... SALES?

When a man courts a woman, or vice versa, the person targeted by these behaviors is made to feel like he or she is the center of the universe. No one else exists. This attention sends a message to System 1 that says, "You are the most special, most important person in the world to me." These behaviors are also effective in sales situations.

When I took over managing the U.S. salesforce at Rauland we suffered many disadvantages. One of them was we weren't courting our customers and one of our strongest competitors was. Their courtship ritual involved flying a group of customers on a private jet to their manufacturing facility that was located in a rustic setting. They were housed in lodges built on the company's property, given spa amenities, and treated to meals cooked by an onsite chef.

This ritual had a name, "Charmed by the farm," and this is an accurate name because it uses charisma's language of enchantment. Customers were unquestionably charmed by the experience. It turned customers into fierce protectors of their brand. I experienced this fierce protectiveness in all of its territorial fury. This company was my competitor in the first chapter's sales-hell challenge. Those customers loved my competitor and me…not so much.

Focus charisma can be a very powerful sales weapon, and my competitor used it to the best of their understanding. However, since they did not understand the emotional causes of the buying-decision-effect, they dulled the sharpness of this blade by combining it with a hard sell at the end of the visit.

Selling is about generating emotions that favor a buying decision, and people don't like to be sold, much less badgered. If my competitor understood the cause-effect relationship of sales, then they would not have done this. This opened a door for us to develop a "courtship ritual" that was even more effective.

One of the first things I did was develop a plant tour that showcased the city of Chicago. A group of customers stayed in a posh hotel right in the midst of top restaurants and shopping. We would take them out on architectural boat tours, and go up to the 95th floor of the Hancock building to enjoy drinks and fantastic views. The evening would end with a dinner at a restaurant that was in a different league from those found in many of the visiting group's hometowns.

The entire time my attention was 100% focused on the customer, and one thing we never did was engage in hard-sell tactics. In fact, one nursing executive jokingly complained she'd spent two days with me and I never tried to sell her one time.

I replied, "Sorry about that. It's all my fault. Have a safe trip home."

You may think, "You weren't doing your job which is to sell, and the nursing executive was stunned and not impressed by this," but I disagree. I was selling in the most effective way, employing the emotional causes of the buying decision. And guess what? She bought our system.

Focusing my time and attention on a customer, and showing them how much I valued them was a powerful expression of charisma. And it wasn't an act. I wasn't faking anything. My customers were very important to me and to my company. Without them, our company would have ceased to exist.

OBSTACLES IN THE WAY OF ATTENTION

Unfortunately, an obstacle prevents us from focusing our attention on others during face-to-face talk, and it's growing larger every day. We have become a world of scatterbrained multitaskers who jump from activity to activity, unable to focus on anything for more than a few seconds.

You've probably seen this on a train, bus or plane—heck, you've even seen this while someone was driving a car: Everyone is texting, surfing the Net, staring at their phones, checking Instagram, Twitter, Facebook or the social media flavor of the moment, oblivious to anything happening around them.

You may be one of these people and, if you are, then you probably believe the myth that you multitask well, and that it is not causing you any problems. Hopefully the following information will change your mind and take you one step closer to that rich world that is occurring all around you:

> Multitasking, when it comes to paying attention, is a myth. The brain naturally focuses on concepts sequentially, one at a time. At first that might sound confusing; at one level the brain does multitask. You can walk and talk at the same time. …Surely this is multitasking. But I am talking about the brain's ability to pay attention. It is the resource you forcibly deploy while trying to listen to a boring lecture at school. It is the activity that collapses as your brain wanders during a tedious presentation at work. This attentional ability is, to put it bluntly, not capable of multitasking.[1]

When it comes to focusing on someone else, you either are or you're not. And when you aren't, System 1 recognizes this because it can see and accurately interpret the smallest, split-second micro-expressions of nonverbal behavior.

WHAT RESEARCH REVEALS ABOUT MULTITASKING

The millennial multitasker would argue, "Look, our generation does this switching of attention exceptionally well, because we've been doing it all of our lives. Your generation doesn't get it, but it should. Haven't you ever heard of the saying, 'Practice makes perfect?' "

This argument has some intuitive appeal. It led Stanford researchers to categorize people, based on their smartphone usage, and to experimentally test their initial hypothesis. They believed the Heavy Media Multitaskers would be able to switch between tasks more quickly and accurately than the Light Media Multitaskers.

Their hypothesis was wrong.

---

[1] John Medina, *Brain Rules* p. 115

In every attentional test the researchers threw at these students, the heavy users did consistently worse than the light users. Sometimes dramatically worse. They weren't as good at filtering out irrelevant information. They couldn't organize their memories as well. And they did worse on every task-switching experiment. Psychologist Eyal Ophir, an author of the study, said of the heavy users: "*They couldn't help thinking about the task they weren't doing.* The high multitaskers are always drawing from all the information in front of them. They can't keep things separate in their minds." This is just the latest illustration of the fact that the brain cannot multitask.[2]

I highlighted the words, "They couldn't help thinking about the task they weren't doing." because I found this to be a frightening depiction of a person who is completely out of touch with the reality of the present moment. They may be here physically, but their mind is always elsewhere and it affects their cognitive performance. The Heavy Media Multitaskers were weaker in several areas: "weren't as good at filtering out irrelevant information," "couldn't organize their memories as well," etc. It appears this embrace of the monkey mind is damaging people's ability to think.

If you are a heavy media multitasker, then don't worry. This chapter and the next one are about getting those cognitive capabilities back, and making them stronger than ever. They will not only improve your "attentional" capabilities, they will also improve your PEM state, your creativity and problem solving. These benefits not only help you with your charisma, they help you manage your sales territory and chart new paths that get you to your destination faster.

THE NEW AGE OBJECTION

Before diving into the subject of meditation I'd like to address a concern that several of my clients have had and that you might share. It is similar to the fear some may have had about the practice of visualization. Namely, it seems to be a New Age practice, and some reject the New Age and everything associated with it.

I understand. I used to be in the New Age. That's where I learned about meditation and visualization. But now I absolutely reject its ideology. For the record, I am a Christian. Yet I still meditate, because nothing about the practice of meditation goes against my beliefs.

---

[2] John Medina, *Brain Rules* p. 115. Emphasis mine.

Both concentration and mindfulness meditation are nothing more than forms of mental exercise for me. They have more in common with jogging than any New Age doctrine.

TWO CATEGORIES OF MEDITATION

Concentration meditation is an exercise aimed at enabling the mind to sustain its single-pointed focus. I believe concentration meditation needs to be mastered prior to practicing mindfulness because, as Dr. Jon Kabat-Zinn notes:

> Concentration is the cornerstone of mindfulness practice....
>
> Concentration can be practiced either hand in hand with mindfulness or separately. In Sanskrit, concentration is called *samadhi*, or "onepointedness."[3]

Dr. Kabat-Zinn then added, "Without some degree of Samadhi, your mindfulness will not be very strong."[4] I agree with him, but I would take his point much further.

Concentration is the foundation for visualization. For if you cannot hold an imagined scene before your mind's eye for more than a few seconds, then the impact of your visualizing will not be much. It is also the foundation for self-talk. It takes focused attention to change the conversation going on in your head. Therefore, if you practice any mental discipline, do not leave this one off your schedule.

If you practice the exercises I've covered, then you will likely become charismatic in one week, but proficiency in meditation takes more time. This makes meditation different from the other exercises in this book. You are exercising your mental muscles, and if they are out of shape, then it will take weeks and sometimes months before you develop your mental fitness.

CONCENTRATION MEDITATION EXERCISES

An exercise that develops the ability to concentrate is as simple as focusing on your breathing:

> Samadhi is developed and deepened by continually bringing the attention back to the breath every time it wanders. ...Our energy is

---

[3] Jon Kabat-Zinn, *Wherever You Go, There You Are: Mindfulness Meditation in Everyday Life* (New York: Hyperion, 1994), p.72.
[4] Kabat-Zinn, p. 72.

directed solely toward experiencing *this* breath coming in, *this* breath going out, or some other single object of attention. With extended practice, the mind tends to become better and better at staying on the breath, or noticing even the earliest impulse to become distracted by something else, and either resisting its pull in the first place and staying on the breath, or quickly returning to it.[5]

Some count their breaths as a way of focusing the mind and building up their ability to concentrate. Here is how I practice breath-counting:

> Breathe deeply into your abdomen, hold your breath for a few seconds, then slowly exhale. With each exhalation you count. You start with the number one and count your exhalations up to the number ten. If you lose focus and forget what number you were on you go back to the starting point and count one, then two, etc.

> Once you reach ten, without making any mistakes, you start counting backwards: nine, eight, seven, etc., back to one.

> When you can easily achieve ten, both forwards and backwards, without mistakes, you graduate to twenty, then thirty, and so on, up to 100. If you ever make it to 100 and back to one without making a mistake, then you will have developed an ability to concentrate that few possess.

CONCENTRATION ON A SEED THOUGHT

As Kabat-Zinn noted, concentration meditation can be focused on breathing, "or some other single object of attention." I agree with him. As a teenager I made a thought or an idea that single object. It would typically be a thought contained in a sentence. I would circle around this thought, look at it from a variety of different angles to try and gain fresh insights into whatever the author was trying to communicate, and unpack the richness of his thought.

What thought should you choose? It can be any thought, phrase, sentence or idea. But if you are new to meditation, then I think it makes sense to pick thoughts that are personally meaningful to you. If it is a thought that you treasure, then it will be easier to hold your attention.

The following is an illustration of a typical meditation session for a beginner. The thought our novice meditator will pursue in this session is a

---

[5] Kabat-Zinn, p. 72.

quote from Henry David Thoreau: "It's not what you look at that matters, it's what you see."

The following are our novice meditator's thoughts as he tries to focus on this one thought and understand it better:

> What is Thoreau trying to say? Obviously we look around ourselves all of the time and miss seeing a lot. We are often mindless and not mindful. What is mindfulness anyway? I need to read that book on mindfulness.
>
> [He catches his attention drifting away and returns to the quote. Mindfulness is related to Thoreau's quote, but getting a book on it is not.]
>
> Thoreau is illustrating a problem. We are surrounded by beauty in the world, by nature's complexity, and yet we do not see it. Wow! If this problem existed back then, then imagine how bad it is now that we have smart phones. I need to charge my smart phone. It's got a 10% charge left.
>
> [He refocuses on the seed thought.]
>
> I wonder if he had this insight when he was living in his cabin at Walden Pond? I read Walden long ago. Some of the chapters were magical, and some were boring.
>
> [He is wandering again. He now tries to make Thoreau's Walden experience relevant to the seed thought.]
>
> Thoreau recorded his observations of nature at Walden Pond. He was present, in the moment, and he saw some things for the first time. Meanwhile, his acute ability to observe the world and experience it in the here and now, revealed to him how so many others were sleepwalking through life.
>
> We look at thousands of things each day and we hardly see anything. As I walk down a tree lined street I rarely see the wind moving through the leaves, the sunlight dancing on them. I need to look up from my smart phone and see the world I live in. I also need to charge my smart phone. It's only got a 10% charge.

Random thoughts, the worries of the day, will force their way into your meditation sessions. Do not be bothered by this. This is normal. But with practice a new normal will emerge. These frequent distractions in the early stages of meditation practice will begin to tail off dramatically after a few weeks. Then, as this happens, your ability to focus your attention and hold it on people, tasks, and so on, will change noticeably.

Once you strengthen your attentional abilities you gain more than just focus charisma. You gain the ability to listen and hear things you used to miss. You see nonverbal cues that help you understand what your customer is feeling and thinking. All of these things make for better sales performance.

THE WALL

What happens when you finally hit a wall, when you can't think of anything new about your seed thought, the object on which you are meditating?

There are several possible paths you can take:

1. The seed thought—"It's not what you look at that matters, it's what you see"—can be related to your personal life by asking yourself, "What am I looking at but not seeing in my personal life? What am I failing to see in my spouse and/or my children, or my relationships with them?"

2. You can relate this seed thought to your work by asking, "What am I looking at but failing to see in my boss, my subordinates, my relationships with them, my primary objectives for the year, or this problem I am trying to solve?"

3. What do I need to see regarding my gifts, and how I am using them?

Concentrating on seed thoughts enables us to improve our ability to focus and gain creative insights into various subjects. It's a win-win exercise on many levels.

UNDERSTANDING THE CREATIVE PROCESS

An important rule governing the creative thinking process can be seen in the way an all-too-typical, creative brainstorming meeting can fail to produce anything creative.

CEO: People I need ideas, fresh ideas. Come on. Get with it.

VP of Sales: How about doubling our sales force to grow our business.

CEO: That's got to be the dumbest idea I've ever heard. Have you ever heard of a P&L? Do you know what EBITDA stands for? Okay people; give me ideas. I need ideas.

How many creative ideas do you think this brainstorming session will now generate? The answer is, "None."

System 1 is the source of those wild out of the box ideas that percolate up from our subconscious minds, and those in the meeting have just seen a VP of Sales being eviscerated for offering up a creative idea. Since System 1 is wired to protect us it will communicate the following strong suggestion: "Keep your mouth shut! Offering out of the box ideas is suicidal. Don't do it!"

There is a simple principle that gives creativity the safe place it needs to play in: Defer judgment. Judgment will have its hour, but only after creative, wild and crazy ideas have emerged. Doubling the sales force may have been a crazy idea that would not work, but that is not what the creative process is trying to accomplish with this over-the-top idea. It is trying to trigger other ideas that might work. For example:

CFO: How about doubling our sales force in our top three markets?

COO: How about reorganizing to support this. We could cut and consolidate in underperforming, small markets and add salespeople to underperforming, large markets.

The point is, by deferring judgment the wildest and craziest ideas can lead to creative solutions that have not previously been considered.

THE CREATIVE CONVERSATION

Here is how I used meditation to generate a creative insight that drove an enormous amount of sales growth. I meditated for several weeks on the following seed thought. It is a meditation that every salesperson would benefit from:

What is the single most important thing I need to be doing to grow sales revenue?

As I focused on this question several dozen pretenders and contenders paraded before my mind's eye. I wrote them down and tried to come up with as many ideas as possible. Volume is an important part of the creative process. If you come up with only three ideas, then they are probably the obvious ones, not the creative ones. But if you force yourself to come up with twenty ideas, then the first three will still be pedestrian, ideas four through ten will be a little better, and the last ideas will probably be the most creative.

I asked others for their opinions to help increase the number of possible solutions. Their viewpoints became a part of my extended meditation. As I gathered these different ideas I deferred judgment.

I call this approach, "Having a creative conversation," because System 2 is asking the question, and then listens. What does the associative machine, System 1, have to say? System 2 was like a sonar pinging the subconscious depths of System 1, to see what lurked below the surface of my awareness.

This question is universally applicable, whether a person is a CEO or a salesperson. For until we know what the number one driver of sales growth is, we cannot focus all of our available energies on it. And if something is the most important driver of sales growth in your territory, then why would you focus a significant amount of your spare time on anything else?

After you assemble all of the possibilities you then subject them to critical analysis. You look at the positives of each potential solution first—you don't want to kill creativity at the first opportunity—and then consider the negatives. Are these issues big enough to disqualify a solution from being the top driver of sales growth? And then, one by one, the ideas are discredited and only the top priority remains.

CREATIVITY, LOST AND FOUND

Creativity is an invaluable ability that we often lose as we grow older. As a kid you allowed your mind to run wild. A stick could become a starship, while a rock could become a meteor, a planet or a death star. Once we stopped listening to the sometimes wild, creative associations generated by System 1, our thinking began to flow down well-worn, predictable channels.

Focusing your mind, stilling its never ending flow of thoughts, may help you hear a creative thought that leads to another and another, and possibly an insight that focuses you on what is truly productive.

The next chapter is closely related to concentration meditation, but with a unique twist that can make your everyday life, and the world around you, come alive in our digitally-distracted age. If you are unfamiliar with mindfulness meditation, you will likely discover that as the world becomes more alive to you, you become more alive in the world.

11

THE POWER OF BEING PRESENT

TRADING THE GOOD FOR THE BAD

Choosing to live mindlessly, instead of mindfully, is like choosing to live in a dilapidated, shotgun shack instead of a luxury home. It is choosing an impoverished experience over one that is full and satisfying.

If we do not live our lives in the reality of the present moment, then we are condemned to live in places that are always at least one step removed from reality: A past that can't come back, a future that is not here, or the virtual reality of non-stop distraction. It may take years, but eventually we will discover how unfulfilling an unreal, virtual life is.

Unfortunately, our amazing System 1 makes a mindless life possible by enabling us to operate on autopilot. We can mindlessly drive for miles and suddenly become aware that we are driving, and wonder how we got to this place on the road. Mindfulness is a rejection of this auto-piloted life.

THE UPSIDE OF MINDFULNESS

Like concentration meditation, the practice of mindfulness also helps us develop our ability to focus, or pay attention:

> … mindfulness is less about spirituality and more about concentration: the ability to quiet your mind, focus your attention on the present, and dismiss any distractions that come your way.[1]

---

[1] Maria Konnikova, The Power of Concentration, NY Times, Dec 15, 2012

When we are fully present our customers can feel it. It is like you are invisibly embracing them. We also do a much better job of listening, because a fully focused mind can pick up on subtle nonverbal signals. Toward the end of the chapter, we will look at mindfulness exercises involving nonverbal behavior.

Mindfulness not only improves our ability to focus, it also optimizes our PEM state. There are over 3,000 research studies on the subject of meditation, and many of them show how mindfulness helps us deal with depression, anxiety, stress, panic and other emotional states that are anti-charismatic.

THE JOY OF MINDFULNESS

One of the most pleasurable aspects of mindfulness is the way it makes everyday life spring to life. James Herriot recorded the following mindfulness experience that reveals how being present in the moment, mindful of what you are experiencing, can be deeply rewarding:

> It was the same every morning but, to me, there was always the feeling of surprise. When I stepped out into the sunshine and the scent of the flowers it was as though I was doing it for the first time. The clear air held a breath of the nearby moorland; after being buried in a city for five years it was difficult to take it all in.
>
> I never hurried over this part. There could be an urgent case waiting but I still took my time.
>
> …And so to the rose garden, then an asparagus bed whose fleshy fingers had grown into tall fronds. Further on were strawberries and raspberries.
>
> Bees were at work among the flowers and the song of blackbirds and thrushes competed with the cawing of the rooks high up in the elms.
>
> Life was full for me.[2]

Mindfulness was a daily experience for Herriot that he cherished and protected. Yes, there were urgent requirements to be met in his veterinary work, but there was also the need for him to be at his best. And so he dallied for a few minutes longer to make sure this joyful experience was carried with him. It made him more effective in his work, not less.

---

[2] James Herriot, *All Creatures Great and Small* (New York: St. Martin's Press, 1972), p. 44.

Henry David Thoreau, the author of *Walden, or Life in the Woods*, once described a mindfulness session in the following way:

> Sometimes, in a summer morning, having taken my accustomed bath, I sat in my sunny doorway from sunrise till noon, rapt in a reverie, amidst the pines and hickories and sumachs, in undisturbed solitude and stillness, while the birds sang around or flitted noiseless through the house, until by the sun falling in at my west window, or the noise of some traveller's wagon on the distant highway, I was reminded of the lapse of time. I grew in those seasons like corn in the night, and they were better than any work of the hands would have been. They were not time subtracted from my life, but so much over and above my usual allowance.[3]

Thoreau was so engaged in the present moment, of being aware of the world he was in, that the passage of time went unnoticed. His path led to the same end as Herriot's: Everyday life became fully alive, a source of joy and happiness. This may seem unrelated to sales, but only insofar as one may think charisma is unrelated to sales. Mindfulness optimizes our PEM state, and this produces the nonverbals that generate charisma. I do not share his beliefs, but must note that at the top of the most charismatic-individual-lists is one of the foremost practitioners of mindfulness: the Dalai Lama.

FORMAL MINDFULNESS EXERCISES

First, I will cover mindfulness practices as they are taught by those who are expert on this topic, to give you an idea of the basics, and then I will show you how I apply it in sales to nonverbal behavior. It is a fun, fascinating exercise that will improve your ability to listen to what a customer is subconsciously saying.

Formal mindfulness exercises can accelerate our growth in the mindfulness discipline. Like many other meditation practices, the following involves breathing. You can begin by sitting comfortably in a chair. Rest your hands on your lap and sit upright but not rigid. An erect posture aids breathing and that will be the focus of your meditation once you are ready to begin. Don't rush. Relax:

> When you're ready, shift your awareness to the changing patterns of sensation in the body as the breath moves in and out. You might

---

[3] Henry David Thoreau, *Walden; or, Life in the Woods* (New York: Clarkson N. Potter, Inc., 1970), p. 243-244.

let your attention rest with the sensations of slight stretching at the belly with each in-breath, and on the sensations of gentle release there with each out-breath. Or you might find that the breath is more obvious to you from the movement of the ribs or from sensations in the chest or throat or nose.

Wherever you find yourself attending to the breath, see what it's like to rest your attention there for the full duration of the in-breath and the full duration of the out-breath, perhaps noticing the slight pauses between breaths.[4]

ACCEPTANCE OR DEFERRING JUDGMENT

Part of mindfulness meditation practice is acceptance, or performing things in a nonjudgmental manner. The author goes on to write:

There's no need here to control the breathing in any way—just let the breath breathe as it does. Even if it seems to be a bit clunky at first, there's no special way you should be breathing. It's simply a matter of gently keeping your attention with the breath—however it is.

As best you can, bring this same attitude of allowing to the rest of your experience—there's nothing to be fixed here, no particular state to be achieved. See what it's like to simply let your experience be your experience—without needing it to be anything other than it is.[5]

Unless you are an experienced meditator you will soon experience a lapse in your concentration. Your mind is elsewhere. But once you notice this you are back in the present moment. Take note of whatever it was you were thinking about and *gently* bring your attention back to your breathing.

Understand that a wandering mind is normal. That's what the mind does during these early stages. It is like you are running wind sprints and the level of exertion requires you to take a breather. It's okay. It's part of the process.

The following instructions, given to the subjects in a mindfulness experiment, nicely sums up this nonjudgmental attitude:

---

[4] Michael Chaskalson, *Mindfulness in Eight Weeks: The Revolutionary Eight-Week Plan to Clear Your Mind and Calm Your Life* (London: Harper Thorsons, 2014). From "Week Two: Mindfulness of the Breath." Page citation unavailable on Kindle edition.

[5] Michael Chaskalson, Week Two: Mindfulness of the Breath

In addition to this focusing of attention, participants were instructed to observe other mental experiences, arising thoughts, feelings or sensations, trying not to judge or evaluate them, and maintain a curious, non-elaborating attitude toward them.[6]

A major theme in mindfulness meditation is self-acceptance. We accept ourselves just as we are at that moment. We try and avoid the tendency of beating ourselves up at all, much less at every opportunity. But if we notice how we are being unduly harsh on ourselves, we need to note this observation with the same degree of acceptance. If that is where we are, then duly noted.

We might think, "Here I am trying to be present and I am everywhere but right here, right now. This exercise is so ridiculously simple and I can't even do it for one minute. Either I'm a joke or this exercise is a joke!" Relax when this happens. Look at this judgmental response, accept it and let it go. When it occurs again, observe it, accept it, and let it go.

WHAT DO I DO WITH THIS UGLY MESS?

Mindfulness can unearth subconscious issues that aren't being dealt with. While we are mindful, these troubling emotions and thoughts can go on parade before our mind's eye. There they are, emerging from their hiding places in all of their imperfect glory. What are we to do with this ugly mess we've uncovered?

Dr. Kabat-Zinn suggested this exercise, and it illustrates how mindfulness can be the first stage of a two-phase process when it comes to solving problems:

Try: Stopping, sitting down, and becoming aware of your breathing once in a while throughout the day. It can be for five minutes, or even five seconds. Let go into full acceptance of the present moment, including how you are feeling and what you perceive to be happening. For these moments, don't try to change anything at all, just breathe and let go. Breathe and let be. Die to having to have anything be different in this moment; in your mind and in your heart, give yourself permission to allow this moment to be exactly as it is, and allow yourself to be exactly as you are.

---

[6] Moore, A., Gruber, T, Derose, J., Malinowski, P. "Regular, brief mindfulness meditation practice improve electrophysiological makers of attentional control," Front. Hum. Neurosci., 10 February 2012 | http://dx.doi.org/10.3389/fnhum.2012.00018

Then, when you're ready, move in the direction your heart tells you to go, mindfully and with resolution.[7]

It helps to understand that mindfulness is not a competition. There is no judge, other than perhaps ourselves, who will give us a mindfulness prize or declare we finished last. Once we start competing with ourselves, or some presumed standard, we are focused on achievement, the future prize, and not the moment.

So, in meditation practice, the best way to get somewhere is to let go of trying to get anywhere at all.[8]

MINDFUL OF NONVERBAL BEHAVIORS

To enter the top echelon of sales we need to be powerful senders of nonverbal behaviors. It helps to be able to interpret them as well. A person who is mindful of nonverbal behaviors, who focuses his attention on them, will not miss a customer's slight, subtle pause of hesitation. And that may be a signal that changes the conversation and saves the sale.

One of the best ways I've found to develop the ability to interpret nonverbal behaviors is by watching politicians run for office. These are people who've been acting for most of their adult lives, and some are really good at it, while others are flat-out abysmal.

The first thing I focus on is the presence or absence of charisma in their nonverbal behavior. I look for whether or not a politician is communicating in a way that makes him or her likable, trusted, respected, authoritative, warm, and focused. Or is their appearance insincere, unsettling and generating distrust? Is this candidate comfortable in his own skin, or does he seem rattled by the whole process of campaigning, responding to tough interview questions, and the like?

THE NONVERBAL ELECTION IN 2016

Here is an example of how this nonverbal observation and interpretation exercise played out during the contentious 2016 presidential nomination. I will limit my observations to just one candidate: Jeb Bush.

He was the early favorite to win the presidential nomination according to many pundits for many reasons. First and foremost, he had the money, a

---

[7] Jon Kabat-Zinn, p. 12. Emphasis mine.
[8] Jon Kabat-Zinn, p. 15.

political record of success as the Governor of the State of Florida, name recognition, and the support of the Republican machine.

Yet, after spending $100 million in a matter of days, he finished sixth in Iowa, garnering 3% of the vote. He finished fourth in New Hampshire with 11% of the vote, and fourth in South Carolina with a mere 8% of the vote. After South Carolina, just three primaries into the nominating process, he called it quits. He was like a fire pit into which donors could throw their money, if they wanted to, and fewer donors wanted to after his third and last showing.

The reason why he failed was as obvious as the expression on his face.[9] He simply had the worst nonverbal behaviors of any candidate I've ever seen. No one else comes close. What follows are my impressions of how the man appeared. This appearance may be 180 degrees different from the way he actually is as a person. But in sales, job interviews and presidential elections, how we are perceived is the driver of decisions.

When presidential candidate, Donald Trump, called him "low-energy" Jeb Bush the name stuck. His nonverbals were listless. His facial expression made him appear to be suffering from chronic pain. Campaigning seemed like self-torture for Jeb Bush. He rarely looked comfortable in his own skin.

Worse yet, he seemed wimpy and utterly lacking in authority. In the political field, where all-strength and no-warmth charisma can be effective, this may be a fatal flaw.

His performance shows how money, name recognition, backing by a powerful political machine, and a past history of political success are not enough to overcome a nonverbal voice that seems to be saying, "I'm not capable of doing the job."

If you are away from the campaign season, then watch a show where people are subjected to hard interviews. "Sixty Minutes," the legendary news program, used to specialize in this with Mike Wallace, but any interviewing show where hard questions are asked is fine. Once tuned in, watch the changing nonverbal expressions of the guest and the host. You will soon become sensitive to the emotions they are expressing.

---

[9] https://www.youtube.com/watch?v=7yHckRTkcZg. This is a link to a video entitled, "Jeb Bush Worst Moments." This video compilation actually focuses on his nonverbal behavior to some degree, and if you watch it you will see how he could never win the presidential nomination. No matter how great Jeb Bush may or may not be, he simply did not look cut out for the rigors of the job.

Developing this skill will help you read and understand the customer who is in front of you.

INFORMAL, EVERYDAY MINDFULNESS

In everyday mindfulness we begin to notice all of the wonders that are around us during the common hours of our day. We do this by being completely present in whatever it is we are doing, enriching the most prosaic moments through mindfulness.

Eating is an exercise that benefits from mindfulness. It makes us eat slower, attend to the flavors and texture of our food, and actually taste it in all its richness for perhaps the first time.

Any automatic task can become an exercise in mindfulness. Take showers, for example. As System 1 takes over the act of bathing, our minds launch past our shower, to go over to-do lists and whatnot.

The classic shower scenario is this: We turn off the water and all of the sudden enter the present and wonder, "Did I wash my hair?" or, "Did I rinse the cream rinse from my hair?"

A mindful shower attends to the sensations that are occurring at each moment. The water spraying down on our head and shoulders and coursing down our body, the bar of soap as it moves across our skin and its smell, the splashing sounds of the water and the way this changes as we move.

There are many other activities that can be the basis of mindfulness exercises. Experiment with them and understand that one becomes mindful by practicing mindfulness.

IN CONCLUSION

Focus. We cannot be charismatic to the person in front of us without the ability to focus our attention on him. Doing so communicates, "You are the center of my attention. You are what really matters most to me at this moment." And that message is very attractive.

It may seem like I've just given you a lot of work. You may think, "How will I ever be able to squeeze all of this into my already busy day?" The next chapter will show just how easy it is.

12

THE CHARISMA
EXERCISE SCHEDULE

MAKING IT WORK

The guiding principle of using these charisma exercises efficiently is this: Combine them to save time. For example, visualization and positive self talk go perfectly together and using them in combination takes little time. I believe visualization, combined with positive self-talk, for ten minutes each day is all you need to become charismatic. If you want to become charismatic in one week, then do this twice a day.

After it becomes more or less habitual, still perform these exercises prior to a major presentation. In fact, I would increase the amount of time I spent on these exercises in the days leading up to one. I want to be operating at my optimum level when presenting and, like rehearsing, I find these exercises increase my confidence.

AEROBIC EXERCISE AND MEDITATION

First, I will assume you exercise in some capacity. If not, then I highly recommend that you start doing so for the sake of your physical, emotional and mental health. Aerobic exercise is like a wonder drug that optimizes your PEM state. If you don't like running, then please insert your preferred form of aerobic exercise in place of running, but I will use the example of running because it is one of the most widely used forms of aerobic exercise.

(Again, be safe. If you are not currently exercising then buy a heart rate monitor and slowly go from walking, to walking fast, to jogging, to running, to running intervals. But remember, moving up this chain of progression too quickly can be very detrimental to your health.)

Until I combined aerobic exercise and meditation, I used to dread running on a treadmill. Now I prefer it, because it makes this time of exercising fly by. I start by running for about five minutes at a slow pace. During this time I practice mindfulness meditation.

I mindfully pay attention to my body, particularly my breathing and how it slowly begins to accelerate. I pay attention to my feet striking the treadmill and how each footfall feels. Then I attend to my legs, checking on the shins, knees, hips, and so on. How is my posture? Am I relaxed or running a little stiffly.

Then, when my warm up is over I start doing interval training for about twenty minutes. The intervals vary, but I typically run hard for five minutes and walk for two minutes. I repeat this three times. And sometimes the last interval involves running slower at an incline.

I run varying lengths of time during my interval training from a faster-paced two-minute interval, to a slower-paced eight-minute interval. During the running segment of the interval work I count my breaths. This is a type of samadhi, or concentration meditation. For example, when I am running a five-minute interval I count each exhalation from one to seventy. Once I reach seventy I start counting backwards, sixty-nine, sixty-eight, etc. I choose the number seventy because I am able to finish the cycle of counting forward and backward before the five minutes is up.

If I miss a number, or forget a breath, or find myself wandering lost in thought, then I have to go back to one and count forward, two, three, etc. If this happens during your interval, you will have less time before the speed segment is up. So, I simply look to see how much time is left in this interval and adopt a lower number target. For example, if I have two minutes left in the segment, then I count to twenty-five and back to one. I reduce the number because I want this counting exercise to be finished by the time the speed segment is completed.

I then return to mindfulness meditation after the counting is completed and remain mindful during the times I am walking between intervals. How is my body responding to this? I pay attention to the various parts of my body and my breathing.

I repeat this process two more times, and walk for five minutes to cool down (one minute at four mph, two minutes at three mph and two minutes at two and one-half mph). I practice mindfulness during this cool-down phase to monitor how my body is recovering. The entire aerobic-meditation program takes around thirty minutes.

I run three days a week with a day off in between each run. Your body needs time to recover from high-intensity interval training. When time allows, I try to add strength training after each run, or during the days when I am not running.

If you are not a runner, then you can combine speed walking, biking, using an elliptical, or any other form of aerobic exercise, with breath counting. While exercising you simply count your breaths to ten, twenty, thirty, or a 100, and then count backwards to one.

SCHEDULE

A schedule for these exercises might look like this:

MONDAY:

Aerobic exercise combined with concentration and mindfulness meditation (thirty minutes).

After exercising, you may need time to cool down before taking a shower. Practice visualization and positive self-talk while cooling down (5-10 minutes).

TUESDAY:

Visualization and positive self-talk (five-to-ten minutes).

WEDNESDAY:

Aerobic exercise combined with meditation (thirty minutes).

Visualization and positive self-talk (five-to-ten minutes)

THURSDAY:

Visualization and positive self-talk (five-to-ten minutes).

FRIDAY:

Aerobic exercise, combined with meditation (thirty minutes).

Visualization and positive self-talk (five-to-ten minutes).

SATURDAY:

Meditation on a seed thought (eventually work up to thirty minutes).

THE GOAL

The goal of these exercises is to remake your nonverbal self in the image of charisma. It is the image of optimal health. Sick and tired people are not charismatic, but people who radiate vitality are.

These exercises will help you gain control of your nonverbal behavior, resulting in charisma, and they will help you accomplish so much more. They will improve your energy level, your mood, your ability to cope with the stresses of everyday life, and your ability to think with a razor-sharp focus. In short, they will enable you to operate at your very best at whatever you do.

In the next section we will cover some of the ways our words can be invested with emotional power and how we can make these words even more powerful by the way we speak them.

PART THREE

Verbal Charisma

13

THE POWER OF WORDS

BANANAS   VOMIT

I open this chapter with the above two words because they enabled me to experience System 1 in a way that I'll never forget.

I was reading Daniel Kahneman's *Thinking, Fast and Slow*, where these words appear, and when I read the word "vomit," I felt a twinge of anger. I turned away from the book in disgust and thought, "He did not need to write this vulgar word."

He went on to write the following words that made me wonder if he was sitting next to me:

> A lot happened to you during the last second or two. You experienced some unpleasant images and memories. Your face twisted slightly in an expression of disgust, and you may have pushed your book imperceptibly farther away. Your heart rate increased, the hair on your arms rose a little, and your sweat glands were activated. In short, you responded to the disgusting word with an attenuated version of how you would react to the actual event. All of this was completely automatic, beyond your control.[1]

In short, I had experienced System 1, the effortless, automatic, subconscious mental system. His description of my response to these words was amazingly accurate, and they likely described your response as well. This means that System 1 may not communicate with words, but it

---

[1] Kahneman, p. 50.

possesses a large vocabulary in its model of the world and can powerfully respond to them.

You've just experienced System 1's response to these words. Now let's consider how System 2 might rationally respond to them:

> Bananas: An excellent source of potassium. Easily digested. A fast, easily accessible source of glucose favored by marathon runners.

> Vomit: An excellent way to rid the body of poisons or prevent you from consuming a fatal dose of poison. For example, prior to alcohol poisoning most people vomit, or pass out, and thereby avoid dying from an overdose.

The cold, rational mind looks at the word "vomit" like a biology teacher looks at a dissected frog. It does not emotionally react to these words because it is rational. But it is slower to respond and, therefore, System 1's lightning-fast, emotional response to this word is the one we experience first and foremost.

System 1's response shows us that words can generate an emotional response that, like nonverbal charisma, can move people in mysterious ways.

OUR MODEL OF THE WORLD

When we saw the words "bananas" and "vomit," other nonconscious processes took place as System 1 tried to update our model of the world. It saw bananas first and tried to develop a narrative that made sense of these two words. "Do bananas cause vomit?" Kahneman continues describing the response of System 1:

> As a result, you are experiencing a temporary aversion to bananas (don't worry, it will pass).

> ...In a second or so you accomplished, automatically and unconsciously, a remarkable feat. Starting from a completely unexpected event, your System 1 made as much sense as possible of the situation—two simple words, oddly juxtaposed—by linking the words in a causal story....[2]

This is an important point. When System 1 updates its model of the world it constructs causal stories, narratives, or schema that attempt to account

---

[2] Kahneman, pp. 50, 51.

for the world we encounter. It is one of the reasons why stories resonate so deeply in the human mind. Stories are basically words that follow the way our minds work.

Before leaving "bananas" and "vomit" I'd like to touch on one other important point that Kahneman makes:

> An odd feature of what happened is that your System 1 treated the mere conjunction of two words as representations of reality. Your body reacted in an attenuated replica of a reaction to the real thing, and the emotional response and physical recoil were part of the interpretation of the event. As cognitive scientists have emphasized in recent years, cognition is embodied: you think with your body, not only with your brain.[3]

Cognition is embodied. The body affects the brain and the brain affects the body. We've seen this mind-body connection at work in aerobic exercise, meditation, visualization, and so on. We see it in the way our bodies, and their nonverbal behaviors, affect the way people feel about us and how we are perceived.

Now we will look at the power of our words to generate emotions that move customers toward making a buying decision.

METAPHORICAL LANGUAGE

Metaphors compare two unlike things without using the words "like" or "as." It is a figurative way of speaking that is typically rich in imagery.

"The eyes are the windows of the soul," is a well-known metaphor. The fact that it has been repeated for centuries sums up the power of a metaphor. Like a good story, good metaphors tend to stick.

Metaphors can make poetry memorable and magical. William Butler Yeats was a poet who wrote some of his best verse after he was sixty years old. This is not the norm. Typically a poet's best days are behind him well before he turns fifty.

Quite naturally, aging became a theme in Yeats's later poetry and his metaphor describing an old man is memorable: "an aged man is but a paltry thing, a ragged coat upon a stick."[4] The image of an old man being a

---

[3] Kahneman, p. 51.
[4] William Butler Yeats, *Sailing to Byzantium.*

scarecrow has a way of staying with you, and that is what good metaphors do.

How can you use metaphors in sales? They can be verbal images that are repeated during the course of a presentation. For example, let's say you sell a technology that is not incredibly flashy, but offers durability and stability. You might describe this benefit in the following way:

> All of the systems you are considering are technology platforms, and your workflow applications will rest on one of them. What is the most important quality a platform like this can possess? Stability. Because if the platform is unstable, and it crashes, then you may lose critical applications just when you need them most.

> Our platform is a rock. And when you're building a house you build it on a rock and not sand. Critical applications should rest on a stable platform, because they will be there when you need them. Our state of the art system is the most stable platform in the industry and it, along with our service department, can be the rock that your system rests on.

CLEAR WORDS IN A CHARISMATIC MOUTH

As far as the conquest of Europe was concerned, England was the only significant obstacle still standing in the way of Adolph Hitler. The previous Prime Minister, Neville Chamberlain, was a man who was not up to the task of confronting this shrewd and ruthless psychopath, but Winston Churchill was.

He was not a dashing figure. Dumpy would be a more accurate description. But he had a charismatic voice—deep, rich and resonant—and he used it to deliver words that are still fresh more than seventy years later. When simple, clear language is spoken by a powerful voice the effect can be magical. (We will look at "The Power of Your Voice" in Chapter 17.)

Allow me to set the stage for one of his more memorable addresses to the people of the United Kingdom:

> England's army was being pushed back into the sea. Over 300,000 men were on or near the beaches of France awaiting ships to transport them to safety so that they might live and fight another day. The hope was that as many as 30,000-40,000 might be saved. But with the seas calm, and with the English navy joined by hundreds of merchant seamen, over 335,000 men were evacuated.

He addressed this in his speech and concluded it with these words:

> We shall go on to the end, we shall fight in France, we shall fight on the seas and oceans, we shall fight with growing confidence and growing strength in the air, we shall defend our Island, whatever the cost may be, we shall fight on the beaches, we shall fight on the landing grounds, we shall fight in the fields and in the streets, we shall fight in the hills; we shall never surrender....

There are some important style points that are worth noting. His words are simple and easy to understand. Clear English is far more powerful than pretentious, puffed-up English. There are so many examples of this, but I will use three:

> To be or not to be. (*Hamlet*, William Shakespeare)
>
> Jesus wept. (*The Gospel According to John*)
>
> If you want a picture of the future, imagine a boot stamping on a human face—forever. (*1984*, George Orwell).

The first two examples are models of clarity and concision. The last example shows the emotional power simple language can achieve. I remember reading those words long ago, and I've never forgotten them. This was Orwell's simple, brutal description of the nature of Big Brother, the totalitarian state.

"Okay," I can hear you thinking, "but I'm in sales. I'm not trying to rally a nation to resist an army that can't seem to be beaten. I'm just trying to sell a product. Give me a break."

The power of these techniques work in sales just as they work in leadership, in coaching, wherever.

I remember watching regions within a national sales force playing competitive games of volleyball. One team, the Nashville region, was behind. They were talented, but seemed to lack self-belief and motivation. I was in the background and kept yelling every few minutes, "Get hot Nashville! Get hot!" As they started to score they started to shout, "Get hot! Get hot!" amongst themselves.

Simple. Primal. Repetitive. It struck a chord in them and elicited an emotional response. And yes, they came from behind and won the game.

REDUCE THE IDEA TO A PHRASE AND REPEAT IT

The following experiment shows how repetition can be psychologically powerful. It results in something called the "mere exposure effect," the label describing the way repeated exposure to something can make a stimulus both acceptable and likable:

> An ad box appeared on the front page of a university newspaper and it had a Turkish sounding word in it. Sometimes the word was ikitaf, while other times it was saricik, kadirga, nansoma, and biwonjni. One of these words appeared twenty-five times, while the others only appeared ten, five, two or one time.
>
> After the words stopped appearing members in the university community received questionnaires asking whether each word meant something good or bad. The words appearing more frequently were rated much more favorably than the words appearing only once or twice. This experiment has been replicated using faces and Chinese ideographs.[5]

These made-up words were neither good nor bad, but repeated exposure made one word appear to be more acceptable than the other. Imagine what the power of repetition will do for words that are not made up.

In Churchill's speech the phrase "we shall fight" is repeated many times. It grows in power with each repetition. It is a simple phrase that is artfully used. It paints a picture of resistance throughout the country, from beaches to hillsides. It also sums up the central idea of his speech: We may have suffered setbacks, and we will likely suffer more, but we will never stop fighting so long as we have breath.

Through words—a simple phrase and word pictures—Churchill was able to generate emotions like courage, hope and the desire to fight to the very end. As salespeople we need to use words to generate emotions as well, and phrases can help achieve this end.

A simple, pedestrian phrase that I would repeat throughout a presentation on our reporting software was, "It's tough to improve what you can't measure." This phrase might be used, and also rephrased, as follows:

> This module tracks how fast you are turning over rooms. It can let you know if you are becoming more efficient in this process or less. And that's important, because it's tough to improve what you can't measure.

---

[5] Tom Payne, *The Path to Job Search Success*, (CreateSpace Independent Publishing Platform, 2015), p. 20. Many of the ideas in *Selling With Charisma* can be found in embryonic form in this book that I wrote to assist jobseekers.

How fast are you responding to alarms? Are they being ignored because of alarm fatigue? How would you know if you can't measure this? And if you can't measure it, then it would be tough to improve it and have any assurance that you have improved it.

Our competitors also had decent software generating reports, but did their measurements lead to improvement? Probably. But by continually repeating my phrase the perception of our package of reports changed. They went from being a potentially nice add-on to becoming a strategic addition to their quest for productivity.

The power of repetition can be seen in other famous speeches like Dr. Martin Luther King, Jr.'s "I Have a Dream" speech. "I have a dream" is a simple phrase that introduced his vision of the end of racial segregation. He could have said, "I have a vision," but that sounds too removed from the lives of everyday people. "I have a strategy," is too cerebral. It might generate thought but not movement. "I have a dream" is simpler, easier to understand, easier to relate to, more emotional and, therefore, more powerful. And he repeated it several times.

Find your phrase. Base it on a differentiating strength of your product or service. Use simple words, and then repeat it throughout your presentation.

Words are powerful, and I've found no more powerful use of words than differentiation. If you master this technique, and deliver it with nonverbal charisma, then prepare to watch your sales soar.

14

THE POWER OF DIFFERENTIATION

NOT FIRST, OR LAST, BUT UNINVITED

At the beginning of my career with Rauland, a large, respected hospital network on the West Coast sent a "Request For Information" to all of our competitors. We weren't even included on this initial list. I thought, "Yikes! We aren't even being invited to the dance." We were in the depressing category of "irrelevant and ignored."

By using differentiation we were not only able to muscle our way onto the list of competitors, we were able to win this order to install systems in two of their hospitals for around $5 million. Had we not used differentiation we probably would not have been allowed to compete.

From a verbal perspective, differentiation is the most emotionally powerful tool a salesperson can use. It is the one technique that elevates your offering and subtly knocks down your competitor's offering. All other techniques merely elevate your own offering. Differentiation, therefore, increases the distance between you and your competitors better than any other technique.

It is a verbal generator of one of the most powerful emotions there is: fear. It generates the emotion that motivated IT to buy IBM mainframes. The difference between IBM and the competitive systems is you don't get fired when you buy IBM.

Differentiation-induced fear is what enabled me to turn around the sales-hell situation in the first chapter. It revealed how the product they favored could not do what they wanted it to do, but ours could. They now feared buying a system that was not capable of delivering much-wanted solutions to communication problems. And remember, this incredibly hostile audience did not accuse me of bashing, or ask me to stop talking about the competitor. Based on my experience, when differentiation is delivered with charisma it can safely occur anywhere.

AT CARD FIFTY

During the sales training course I instinctively knew how critical my nonverbal behavior was when it came to differentiating, and I stressed the following message to my training classes:

> To avoid offending, or the appearance of bashing, it is important to follow these rules during a presentation:
>
> 1. Tone is all-important. When differentiating I adopt an almost clinically dispassionate voice, because I know an emotional tone will evoke an emotional response. If I sneeringly say, "Their product can become unstable when it tries to handle heavy data traffic, and I will tell you why," then the audience will immediately think I am bashing the competitor. If I say the exact same words in a dispassionate voice, they are not offended at all. So, do not use an emotional tone when making these product comparisons.[1]

Unfortunately, I did not train them in how to control their nonverbal behavior, and some of them were later accused of bashing the competition, while I never was.

This shows how I was at card fifty. I had a gut feeling that nonverbal behavior was critical to this differentiating process, but I was unaware of how absolutely essential it was. If I had known this, I would have made my visualization and self-talk exercises part of the training class.

ACCUSED OF BASHING

There is a reason why salespeople are always told, "Don't speak about the competition." It is because most people do it poorly and it explodes in their face. I now return to the story I briefly referenced in the first chapter.

---

[1] Tom Payne, *The Causes of Sales Success: The Key to Navigating the Maze of Sales* (Chicago: EGS Publishing, 2012), p. 73.

A salesperson named Vicki, who I had trained, made a clumsy stab at differentiation and a decision influencer, Barbara, said in a withering tone, "Listen here. You may get mileage out of bashing the competition elsewhere, but you will get nowhere with me. Is that understood?" She meekly said, "Yes," and then waited an eternity for that moment to pass.

Why did Vicki fail?

I believe the primary reason Vicki failed is because she sometimes had an arrogant tone and was frequently judgmental. I'd seen it expressed before in casual conversations. When you project haughtiness in sales you are begging to be knocked down a peg, and in this sales circumstance the nurse obliged.

I trained Vicki to differentiate, but I failed to teach her how to control her nonverbal behavior and express kindness and warmth. Hence, her anti-charisma guaranteed her words would be forcefully rejected, while my charisma virtually guaranteed my words would be accepted.

BLINK, RETHINK, UH OH!

When you are selling a system that can cost millions of dollars there are several presentations that will be made, sometimes over the course of a few years. In the case of the hospital where Barbara worked as a nurse, it was nearing a decision and so, just a week later, she came to see a second presentation at the distributor's showroom, accompanied by the rest of the decision-making contingent.

I was scheduled to present. The question was, "Should I differentiate?" I hate to admit it, but I blinked while staring at the prospect of differentiating to Barbara. I thought it would be a bad idea since she was sensitized to "bashing." She might now have a mindset that we are a company of bashers and differentiating might reinforce this mindset and generate negative emotions. So, I removed all differentiating slides, stories, etc., from the presentation.

Then, shortly before the customer group arrived, I found out Barbara was not going to attend this presentation. I quickly changed my presentation back to its original, differentiating format, because I felt differentiation offered us the best chance for success. This was a three-hospital system in the backyard of an entrenched competitor and winning this account would not be easy. My presentation with all of its differentiating slides was on the screen awaiting the arrival of our guests when Barbara walked through the door with the rest of the group. We had been misinformed regarding her absence.

What was I to do? They were in the room where the presentation was being given. I could not change it in front of them. Therefore, I differentiated our product, followed the principles outlined in this chapter and this, along with the efforts of others, won the sale. And I was not accused of bashing.

This highlights the importance of charisma—something I possessed and Vicki did not. On top of this, I highly recommend taking the following preliminary steps prior to differentiating.

STEP 1: SECURING THE RIGHT TO DIFFERENTIATE

I always begin by selling the customer on the need to make a product comparison, whether the crowd appears to be friendly or hostile, because we can never be 100% certain what their attitude is.

I usually start by asking them, "Can you tell me the differences between the products?"

This question works for me no matter how they answer it. Suppose they say, "No." I then respond:

> If you don't know the differences between the competitive systems at the end of this evaluation, then you might as well flip a coin, because until you know their differences both products will appear to be the same. We find that our customers appreciate being told the differences, because it helps them make an informed decision at the end of this process.

In the rare cases when the customer responds, "Yes, we know some of the differences." I then ask, "And what are they?" In almost every case I have found them to be differences favoring the competitive product, which leads me to reply:

> I can tell by the nature of these differences that our competitor has been doing his job and that is telling you how our products are different. To make an informed decision you need to know these differences, so I will continue the process he began, and tell you about some of the important differences he might not have mentioned.

If they were ever to mention differences that favored us, I would congratulate them for knowing some, and ask if they knew any others. Once they exhausted their list, I would reply:

> Excellent! You've almost done my job for me. When we pose this same question to most of our other customers we find they cannot

give us a single difference, and you've named three. Now I am happy to tell you there are several other powerful and important solutions our product offers that the competitive products do not. I think you will find they make our system even more valuable.

There are other ways to secure the right to differentiate, and I've used all of them at different times to keep my selling fresh. I would sometimes illustrate the evaluation process, and the problems it causes:

We have found that after a customer has listened to four or five of these presentations all of the facts become a blur. They are now faced with making a very expensive decision, and they are not sure which system does what. What they tell us helps them is for us to spell out the differences as clearly as possible, so that they can then research these areas on their own to ensure these differences are real; and that is what I am going to be doing in my presentation.

This is quickly followed by one of the most important steps you can take prior to differentiating.

STEP 2: DEVELOP THE MINDSET

I stumbled upon this idea of mindsets while reading a CIA manual that can be found online. To restate the three rules governing mindsets:

1. They form quickly.
2. They resist change.
3. They assimilate all new incoming data to fit the preexisting image.

What struck me about this psychological mechanism was its almost irresistible power. Even though the CIA's analysts are aware of this tendency of the mind, they still fall into this mental trap of developing mindsets that influence their evaluation of intelligence.[2] Therefore, knowledge of this process does not prevent it from still working in many cases, if not most.

---

[2] Richards J. Heuer, Jr., *Psychology of Intelligence Analysis,* (Center for the Study of Intelligence, CIA, 1999), p. 1. The book begins with this summary statement introducing *Chapter One, Thinking About Thinking*: "Of the diverse problems that impede accurate intelligence analysis, those inherent in human mental processes are surely among the most important and most difficult to deal with. Intelligence analysis is fundamentally a mental process, but understanding this process is hindered by the lack of conscious awareness of the workings of our own minds."

Creating this differentiation-mindset never involves saying something like, "I am an honest broker of objective information." Instead, we create this mindset by saying things that suggest we are such a person. All of our words and actions that follow will then reinforce this image.

After securing the right to differentiate, I would say something like:

> In this comparison I will be presenting the facts as objectively as possible. [True.] This information is based on the latest marketing research that we have [True.] and if you know or believe anything I say to be untrue, then please interrupt me and let's discuss it. The reason I ask you to do this is because you have an advantage that I don't. Our competitor will tell you the latest and greatest developments about his product, but he will not tell me, so some of what I tell you may have changed without our being aware of it.

When you tell the customer about a difference between the two products you must always be honest and accurate. Always. And you really do want to know if you have misstated something, because if you have, and you continue to do so in other presentations, it will diminish your presentation's effectiveness.

It is disarming to invite a customer to interrupt your presentation to tell you when you are wrong, or when they think you might be. It lets them know that you are interested in engaging in an open and honest dialogue and this helps create the mindset that you are the honest broker of objective information. What is so ironic is the way this cold, rational approach can generate such hot, powerful emotional responses.

STEP 3: THE DIFFERENTIATION PRESENTATION

To avoid offending, or the appearance of bashing, it is important to follow these rules during a presentation:

1. As I previously noted, tone is all-important. Do not use an emotional tone when making these product comparisons.

2. Never overstate the facts. Differentiation does not go for the carotid-artery to inflict a quick kill. It is more like inflicting the death of a thousand cuts. In effective differentiation no one point is sufficient to win the day when up against a favored competitor, but after inflicting numerous wounds the competitor slowly begins to stumble and fall. Here is an example of what I mean by understating the facts:

Suppose a competitor is misleadingly telling a customer that it can make its product integrate with another important system, but there is no evidence that it can and plenty of evidence that it cannot. Even if I believe their product lacks a capability they are touting, I never say, "Their system cannot do this. If they have told you this, then they are misleading you." This sort of direct language is too confrontational and emotional and it can generate pushback from the customer, and accusations of bashing.

Instead I say, "I know of no place in the country where this integration has been made to work, and if you have a specific reference site where you have <u>seen</u> this integration work, then please let me know so that I can change what I say in my presentations. But if you haven't seen this integration working in a reference center, then please make sure that you do before you attribute to their product benefits I don't believe it possesses."

Does this not accomplish the same thing as the blunter statement? No, it accomplishes much more. The blunt statement may have the customer silently thinking, "But our rep told us it works in a business on the east coast. This guy doesn't know what he's talking about." The softer statement will have them wondering, "I haven't actually seen it work and I don't think they ever gave us a reference account and contact person to call to check up on this?"

3. Never attack the competitor's salesperson even when he is guilty of telling the most outrageous lies. To do so would be to invite a decision maker to defend him since he is absent and cannot defend himself. When confronted with an obvious lie I ask, "May I ask where you heard this?" If they tell me, "From your competitor." I reply, "The exact opposite is the case, and this fact has been known for several years throughout our industry, so I am very surprised he does not know about this." The customer can draw their own conclusions and it just could be this salesperson is new, or was told the wrong information from their marketing department. I was a salesperson once and have been fed misinformation, so I know it happens.

4. Rehearse extensively prior to differentiating in front of a hostile audience. As you are gently undermining the position of their friend—your competitor—they will be watching you like a hawk.

Can you look them in the eye and speak with a steady, authoritative tone, or does your voice crack with nervousness? The style of your presentation is more important than its substance when it comes to the decisions made by System 1.

5. Be as factually accurate as possible. If you make more than one mistake, the audience will begin to think, "Does this guy know what he is talking about?" For ethical and practical reasons, be accurate and honest.

DIFFERENTIATION BUILDS TRUST

To differentiate is to act like a consultant. To appear to be a consultant generates the emotion of trust. Yes, mentioning the competitor actually fosters a stronger relationship.

I once presented to a customer who favored our competitor, having bought their expensive system before. As I went into the differentiation, she began to see why their system was never able to do some of the things she had always wanted. Also, the competitor never gave her a satisfactory answer about its limitations. She then looked at me and asked, "Why haven't they fixed this?"

Think about this. She is asking a biased salesperson for information about his competitor. This is another example of the way charisma changes the way you are perceived and ushers you into a new reality. I was now being asked a question that she would typically ask a consultant. In other words, I was now less of a salesperson and more of a consultant who was part of her decision making team.

I could have answered in a strong way, tearing my competitor to shreds, but I was differentiating and I did not want to stir up emotions that might push back. So, I responded, "I have no idea why they haven't fixed this. To offer an explanation would be pure speculation on my part."

To which she replied, "Speculate, please."

I then offered her my honest opinion of possible reasons why they had not fixed one of their system's biggest shortcomings. She thanked me and days later became our customer. What is remarkable is the way my product comparison resulted in her treating me as if I was a trusted consultant working for her. Differentiation, when performed well, builds trust, and building trust is one of our primary goals.

Differentiation won the sale in many difficult selling situations, and not just this one. It helped to sell our system to customers who were vocally opposing us up until the moment our final presentation began. One of the more memorable occasions now follows. At every step, this customer's irrational bias was on full display.

"YOU KNOW WHAT I THINK OF YOUR STUFF."

We were trying to break into a city that was one of our top competitor's strongholds. They had a salesperson who had strong relationships with powerful decision makers throughout this city's largest accounts. We found out about an opportunity at one of them, and my Region Manager went to visit it with our distributor.

After this meeting, my Region Manager wrote the following in his call report (all of the names have been changed):

> Harriet [the primary decision maker] arrived 20 minutes late and announced she didn't know why she was even there. …Harriet said she needed the system to have ease of connection and interact well with [one of our competitor's other products].

This competitor's salespeople routinely planted this objection. It was saying, "I require your product to do what I know it cannot do." The story continued to unfold in his call report:

> While there was a conversation between me and another, Harriet leaned over to Jill [the distributor salesperson] and told her "I've met with you several times and you know what I think of your stuff." Interesting comment considering Jill is new to [our distributor] and has never been at [this hospital] before.

> Our chances at winning this project are marginal but the best they have ever been or ever will be.

Marginal chances are what differentiation makes a living off of. During the needs analysis phase that followed, the Region Manager also noted:

> Harriet is a bit of a loose cannon. She gets so caught up into trying to [support] her need to have [our competitor's product that] she can become illogical in her arguments. She doesn't seem to really know [their] system so [she] just locks onto the few key features she seems coached [on]….

Illogical? Did someone say the decision is emotional in nature and not rational?

Again, it is counter-intuitive to enter a situation like this and think, "Let's paint our competitor, who is loved, in a bad light," but it is our only option.

After all, how can a reasoned argument compete against the power of a strong emotional attachment? Try to reason someone out of being in love. It doesn't work, because reason is not strong enough to sever these emotional bonds.

The only thing that has a chance of succeeding is to introduce a more powerful emotion to replace, or overpower, the existing one, and that is what differentiation does. It introduces the emotion of fear, the dread of making a bad decision that will haunt the decision maker for as long as he or she works at that location.

Harriet was now at our corporate headquarters and I was slated to present first. Moments before I spoke Harriet said, "I think your reliability is a problem."

Reliability was one of our product's greatest strengths, and our company had traditionally focused on this benefit. Therefore, Harriet was attempting to remove what she believed to be our primary benefit seconds before I started to present.

She continued, "I pray your [older generation system] dies so we are forced to get rid of it. As it is, it never dies and I'm stuck with this system that can't do what I want or need."

I thought, "This ought to be fun. Here we go."

ESTABLISHING THE MIND SET

I used a slightly different approach to establish the mindset that differentiation was necessary. It went something like this:

> Ultimately, when you make a decision it will be based on the differences between the two systems. They both do very different things. Since this is our first time together, I need to tell you how our product is different from our competitors so that you can make an informed decision.

> My statements will be fact based. I am not interested in slamming my competitor because they are a phenomenal company with phenomenal salespeople. And to make sure it is fact based I would ask you a favor: if at any time you know I am wrong on a point, or even if you think I am, please interrupt me and let me know.

> The reason why I say this is because our marketing department does a great job of gathering information about our competitors, but we do not have a direct line of communication with our

competitors and you do. They may have changed their product and we might not know about it yet. So, let me know if I am off base on something. Okay? Let's get started.

I'm not sure Harriet was ever convinced that our solution was better than the one she favored, but the rest of the decision-making group, who attended our plant tour, must have been because their hospital ended up buying our system.

Differentiation is fun. I imagined Harriet kicking and screaming as her team dragged her toward agreeing to issue us a purchase order.

CONCLUSION

Here is a two-phased plan that will lead to sales success.

> Phase One: Master your nonverbal voice by performing the exercises detailed in Part Two.
>
> Phase Two: Master the art of differentiation.

Words that generate emotion are a form of verbal charisma. They captivate, arouse and sometimes even entertain. This is particularly true of stories, the subject of the next chapter.

15

THE POWER OF STORIES

PIERCING THE MIND FOG

When someone tells us a story it is a ready-made narrative pattern that is stored away in System 1, and it can generate a powerful influence on people for weeks and months. This makes the story a powerful way of conveying a sales message.

How do I know stories can still resonate in the minds of people months later? Because I have personally experienced it and so have my clients. In one instance Carla interviewed for a job and six months later, during a performance review, her manager recounted one of the stories she had told him during her interview. He cited it as the reason why he believed she would turn things around.

Six months later and the story was still influencing him. That is amazing by itself, but place that story in its context and it becomes even more amazing. After all, isn't the job interview one of the unlikeliest places for someone to remember anything?

If you've ever participated in the process of interviewing a group of people, then you've probably experienced the following:

> The first interview is okay. You're early in the process. You still feel strong. The second interview nicks you a bit. Some air starts coming out of the balloon. The interviewees are trying too hard and their self-promotion is off-putting and tiresome. Yet, what are they supposed to do, you tell yourself? That means interview number three will also be a trial of strength, but you are beginning

to grow weary. Interview number four has you looking at the candidate with the 1000-mile stare. The interviewee is in front of you, but you are on a beach somewhere with an umbrella drink. The fifth and final interview helps you remember why you dreaded going through this interviewing process, but at least its over.

In front of you is a pile of five resumes, and you cannot associate a face with any of them. You've entered a mind fog and can barely remember anything of significance from any of the interviews.

But this did not happen to Carla. What she said was remembered long after the interview. So, imagine the impact a story can have on customers during your sales presentation. They go off to decide between you and your competitors and suddenly one of your stories stored away in their subconscious mind emerges. They smile. It was a good story and, more importantly, it reminds them of a key difference between your product and theirs. You are no longer in the room, but you are definitely inside the customer's head, speaking to them, nudging them closer to a buying decision.

Most job-interviewing books recommend telling stories, but they often fall far short in one critical category. They fail to tell the jobseeker how to construct a good story. This is a reckless omission because bad stories— ones that are too long, convoluted or boring—hurt your cause. So by all means, use stories, but only good ones.

Even if you're armed with the knowledge of how to write a good story be prepared for this: Writing a good story is hard work. Most people cannot do it on their own. This is because the act of writing just one good sentence is extremely difficult.

As one of the great prose stylists of the twentieth century put it:

> …Writing is hard work. A clear sentence is no accident. Very few sentences come out right the first time, or even the third time. …If you find that writing is hard, it's because it is hard. It is one of the hardest things that people do.[1]

The difficulty of writing a single, effective sentence is compounded by the need to string several of them together in a way that clearly conveys a good story. If there was one area where my intelligent, well-educated clients struggled it was with the development of stories.

---

[1] William Zinsser, *On Writing Well: An Informal Guide to Writing Non-Fiction* (New York: Harper & Row, Publishers, Inc., 1985), pp. 11, 12.

Embrace the difficulty of this task and give thanks for it. It is a barrier to entry that most of your competitors will never get past, because it will take too much time and effort and they will fail to realize that this is time well spent. For once you have written a story, edited it many times, and can now say it flawlessly, you will possess a gift that keeps giving, presentation after presentation. Now the words you say will be memorable, entertaining and imbued with the power of verbal charisma.

The art of story creation follows a few simple rules. Once you know them and apply them you will be on your way to increasing the distance between you and your competitors.

THE THREE SECTIONS OF A STORY

SECTION 1: HOOK

A story has three sections and each section has a different goal. The first section is the hook, meaning it must hook the attention of the audience and not let them go.

The hook is most powerful when it introduces a seemingly hopeless conflict between the hero and the villain. In a sales story the hero could be the customer at another account who used the product you are selling. The villain would be a seemingly hopeless, or infuriating, problem they overcame.

Powerful stories feature big villains. The more powerful the villain, the better the story. Think of the story of David and Goliath and how this story has captivated audiences throughout the centuries.

In the world of film, *Star Wars* had its Darth Vader. And in *The Exorcist*, a movie that is consistently voted one of the scariest movies of all time, the villain is a demon with supernatural powers.

This idea translates into sales as follows: The larger the obstacle confronting a customer in your story, the more interested your audience will be in its outcome.

If you have a powerful hook, one that grips the imagination, then the words you say will not only lodge a narrative pattern in System 1, it will be a memory that will be readily accessible to System 2 for months.

In the following illustration of an effective story, the salesperson is selling a product that requires servicing. Service is an important part of the total package. So, to highlight his company's service capabilities he starts by framing the story he will soon tell:

> When a hospital is purchasing a life-safety system that is designed to never shut down, service is one of the most important considerations. This system must work every minute of every day, year after year, and that requires maintenance and quick responses to emergency situations.

The first paragraph sets up the story. It establishes the mental frame or mindset that will influence how the story is categorized and interpreted. The mindset it seeks to establish is: "Service is absolutely critical." And then it follows this up with a story that proclaims, "And we are the best service company you can partner with."

His story now begins:

> You might remember how Acme Hospital experienced a crippling lightning strike on Christmas Eve a few years ago. It took down all of their electrical systems. All of them. It was more than just a disaster. Patients died. This was the worst catastrophe they had ever experienced and it happened on the worst possible day.

The story begins by immediately building up the villain, or the problem caused by the lightning strike and the complete loss of power. The bigger the villain, the more compelling the story. To achieve this end, it includes details that are emotionally powerful, "Patients died." It is stated in simple, concise language.

The story continues:

> Just like every other business, we were closed for the Christmas holidays. All of our technicians were at home with their families, but we always have a tech on call. When he received Acme's call for help, he asked questions, determined the magnitude of the problem and took the following steps.

The first section ends with a segue taking us into the next section that details the actions taken by our "hero." It is a tricky section where many stories bog down and become ineffective.

SECTION 2: ACTIONS

The actions taken to overcome the obstacle, or defeat the villain, should be few in number. They primarily serve as a bridge that connects the beginning—the hook—with the end—the payoff. The beginning and the end of a story are the most important sections because we tend to remember what is said first (primacy) and last (recency), and tend to forget what is in the middle.

The narrative loses momentum and interest when too many details are larded on in this second section. So, after you write a first draft of your story focus your editorial energy on whittling this section down to size. If at all possible, limit your actions to three. The above story about the lightning strike now continues with the last sentence followed by the actions taken:

> When he received Acme's call for help, he asked questions, determined the magnitude of the problem and took the following steps.
>
> He knew he would need help so he called another tech to join him at the hospital. Then he loaded up the service truck with lots of extra parts to save time. As it turned out, they needed all of them and more.

The bridge has been built and now we can go to the pay-off.

SECTION 3: PAYOFF

Some people call this section of the story "Results." That is an accurate description, but it fails to emphasize what this section is trying to accomplish. It is more than just reporting an outcome. It is an attempt to offer a satisfying conclusion. If the first two parts of the story are really strong, but the final part is weak, then the story is disappointing and leaves a bad taste.

Here are two guidelines:

> 1. If you don't have a good hook that interests people, then you don't have a story worth telling.
>
> 2. If a story has a weak payoff, then it is not an expression of verbal charisma. It is more like a lukewarm cup of flat beer than a sparkling glass of champagne.

For example, let's say the above story offers the following sad conclusion:

> The two techs were held up by bad weather and arrived after five hours only to discover the electrical system of the hospital was compromised to a degree that made their repair work impossible. So they left and waited for the infrastructure repairs and then returned three days later to fix their system. It took two days to get

it up and running but they finally fixed it and it is still running as good as new.

A key element of good service is speed, and if your story is a tale of delays and fixing a problem after days of waiting, then what good has your story accomplished? None.

Some weak payoffs can be salvaged by adding a few more details. In the above example, the payoff might work if the person telling the story could say the following at the beginning of the payoff: "Within eight hours we installed a temporary system, and this was the most important step we could have taken because of all of the unanticipated delays that followed...."

This story, which is based on a real event, had a satisfying payoff that went like this:

> In less than eight hours all of the problems were identified, compromised parts were replaced, and the database was uploaded. This hospital was fully functional after a catastrophic failure on Christmas Eve eight hours after it occurred. All of their other electrical systems were down for much longer. The hospital was amazed by the speed of our response, and they are still amazed. I called on this hospital about a week ago and they are still talking about how we took care of them.

The pay-off should be:

- To the point.
- Demonstrate the delivery of a benefit or solution to the customer that is highly valued.
- If it can differentiate you from your competitors, or even others who service your customer in different capacities, then be sure to include that detail. In the above example the salesperson includes the telling detail, "All of their other electrical systems were down for much longer." In other words, our service was far superior to everyone else.

In about ninety seconds this story delivered a large quantity of information praising his company's service capability in a way that did not sound like a sales pitch. It is memorable, engaging, entertaining and not what most customers are used to hearing.

THE DATA DUMP

The data-dump is where sales presentations go to die. It is so boring, so difficult to follow that I doubt charisma can overcome it. I invite you to experience the following data-dump, complete with all of the extraneous verbiage that typically clutters the unrehearsed sales pitch:

> We are the best of the best when it comes to service. Our service is 24-7-365. Like I said, the best. We have three fully stocked trucks available, and we've never needed more than these three trucks to be on site anywhere in our territory. And we get there in one hour or less. We used to have two trucks, but we are excited about the way three trucks give us more flexibility, and the way it improves our response times. Our technicians are all factory trained in every system they work on. They've received extensive customer service training. They have a combined tenure of 45 years with our company. It is highly likely they know your hospital's technical staff on a first-name basis. This staff is available to you for the first year at no additional charge. And, I'd like to take a moment to brag on them. They've won awards from the manufacturers they represent in ten of the last ten years.

Blah, blah, blah, blah. In less than a minute I have bombarded your prefrontal cortex with a forgettable data-dump that is best described by one word: boring. Charisma is not the snooze button on a customer's internal alarm clock. It energizes and holds the attention. That is why verbal charisma is such an important complement to its nonverbal cousin.

The data dump is a way of selling against human nature. It is difficult for System 2 to keep up with it. Consequently, it produces the mental state called cognitive strain. This makes the customer's mind suspicious and vigilant. We simply are not wired to process an endless stream of information.

Our goal is to generate a mental state of cognitive ease wherein the customer is relaxed, in a good mood and believes what they hear.

GENERATING COGNITIVE EASE

One of the reasons why stories are so powerful is they generate cognitive ease. When you start to tell a story a person's guard drops. They want to sit back and enjoy the experience. So, System 1 says, "System 2, relax. It's a story. It's something I'm very familiar with. It's safe." And the customer's critical, rational mind is put at ease. It makes them receptive to whatever it is you are telling them.

A lack of clarity causes cognitive strain. Please follow these rules to prevent the generation of this unwanted mental state:

- Use simple language.
- Write your stories down on paper so that you can edit them.
- Repeatedly edit your stories. Every first draft will be bloated. Typically the word count of a first draft can be cut in half.
- While editing your story make clarity a goal. Make sure the sentences communicate the message in a straightforward manner by keeping the sentence structure simple.
- Do not try to say a story off the top of your head. Doing so will produce the mental equivalent of a written first draft. Wordiness and a lack of clarity will be the likely result.
- Read your story out loud while editing. It is like looking at the story from a different perspective. It will help you locate problems you otherwise might miss.
- Through editing and rehearsing your story you will remember it, free of bloat, and will deliver it powerfully.
- If you think it will sound canned—because you've rehearsed it— then you are mistaken. The key to sounding natural is to rehearse until you no longer sound rehearsed. I've rehearsed and delivered stories, presentations and training classes on many occasions. The anonymous feedback the audience gave me never once criticized me for sounding canned.
- Rehearse. Master your material and you will speak with authority and confidence. You will be relaxed, and not struggling to remember the details of the pay-off.

"IS THIS A LONG STORY OR A SHORT STORY?"

Most people look forward to hearing a story until it begins to drone on and on. So, keep your stories short. Most stories can be told in sixty to ninety seconds. If there was a time limit I would place on a story it would be around two minutes. Exceptional storytellers can go on for much longer, but for most of us the two-minute limit is a safe gauge.

Setting a time limit accomplishes several worthwhile goals. It puts a premium on the words being used and motivates the storyteller to eliminate the unnecessary words. This keeps the story moving at a brisk pace, because 60-120 seconds is not a lot of time to tell a story, but it is typically enough. In this perpetually rushed world a brief story possesses the virtue of quickly delivering its rewards. The customer does not dread another long story because you've yet to tell one.

When we tell stories we speak the language of System 1, because it automatically constructs narratives where none exist. We have a primal response to stories because they are a part of our primal being. They speak directly to our emotional mind, System 1.

Stories are one way to differentiate yourself, because few salespeople use them effectively. They also have the virtue of being memorable and entertaining. Like nonverbal charisma, they can help change how you are perceived in favorable ways, and this is also true of the questions we ask, the subject of the next chapter.

16

POWER QUESTIONS

CHANGING HOW YOU ARE PERCEIVED

I'll never forget the Chief Nursing Officer's (CNO) statement to me as we were enjoying dinner with her key staff members. She said, "You really surprised me over the phone." I gave her a puzzled look and asked, "Uh oh. What did I do now?"

"Well you told me that you wanted to ask some questions to get an idea about some of the issues and problems we might be facing prior to our visit, and I thought, 'Oh boy, here comes the questions about how important is this feature and that feature.' You know, the standard sales routine. But you asked me questions about my goals, my vision for the nursing department and I was stunned."

"Is that a good thing or a bad thing?" I asked.

She smiled and said, "It's a good thing. I found it refreshing."

Almost every sales book tells you to ask questions, but as the CNO's response indicates, sometimes these questions can generate a negative perception of the salesperson. What is important, therefore, is not asking the typical salesperson questions, but asking ones that favorably change a customer's perception of you.

THE POWER OF ASKING GOOD QUESTIONS

I was working for a distributor of commodity packaging products and the margins were razor thin. This required every salesperson to produce enough sales to cover their salary and benefits, and one of them wasn't. He was a friendly sort, and smart enough to be a successful salesperson, only he wasn't succeeding. So, I traveled with him to see what it was he would say to his prospects and accounts. He would typically start a sales call by asking:

> Hey Joe, got anything for me to bid on today?

He thought he was serving his company well, beating the bushes, trying to uncover some opportunities, and did not realize this question was killing whatever chances he may have had to succeed.

At first, the question seems harmless, but when we consider it from the customer's perspective, it is anything but. The salesperson thought he was communicating:

> Hey Joe, throw me a bone and I will see if I can shave off a few nickels and save you some money.

He didn't realize he was actually saying:

> Hey Joe, you can probably imagine that since I'm traveling with my boss I need to close some business. Any business. Yes, if you throw me a bone it will create work for you, and the savings I will be able to offer are probably insignificant. Furthermore, what you've got is probably working fine, but still, you gotta help me. Please!

After two performances like this I'd seen enough. The next account we were visiting was a division of 3M. I had to give the kid credit for at least scheduling an appointment that looked like it had potential, but the last thing we needed was one of his repeat performances in front of a professional outfit of their caliber. So, I took him off to the side and made him rehearse a few questions with me, repeatedly, until he memorized them. Then I said, "After our introductions I want you to lead off with these questions."

They were targeted questions that were related to potential problems they might be having with packaging that led to the quarantining of product:

> Do you often quarantine products because of packaging defects?
> Was this quarantining of products a big problem?

After he asked these questions, and a few others we had rehearsed, the engineer turned from the salesperson to me and said, "No one has ever asked me those questions before." He looked back at the salesperson,

"Look, the person you need to see is so and so. Talk to him about this and tell him I sent you."

Why such a strong response? Because we were probably the first company to ask this engineer questions designed to uncover problems relevant to him.

Would a question about a packaging problem affect a CEO so powerfully? Only if he had experienced a packaging problem so large in scale that it threatened quarterly earnings, or the company's quality reputation in the marketplace. In other words, packaging defects are not a big concern for most CEOs, but for this engineer packaging was a big deal. His response confirmed this fact. This is why questions need to be custom-tailored.

The salesperson who asked, "Hey Joe, you got anything for me to bid on today?" was the same salesperson who asked consultative questions to an engineer working for a Fortune 500 company, and who then grew his business by 30% that year. In other words, the problem was not with who the salesperson was, but with his behaviors. Once the behaviors changed (in this case, *questions*), the results were completely different.

Like nonverbal behavior, asking informed and targeted questions can change how a salesperson is perceived. They also uncover what is emotionally important to the customer and this makes effective questioning a vital part of verbal charisma.

THE BEST QUESTIONS

The best questions are the ones that reveal powerful emotional responses. A question I always asked everyone, regardless of a customer's rank, was, "What are your goals?" After they answered this general question I would follow up with a more specific question, "What goals has your boss tasked you to accomplish? Are they same as the ones you've just shared?"

There are two primary reasons why these questions are powerful. First, our goals are tied to the powerful emotion of hope. What does the customer *hope* to accomplish this year?

Second, a boss's goals are typically tied to incentive pay or rewards. When you uncover a person's incentive-related goals it enables you to show someone how your product or service can help him achieve annual goals that are enriching.

Would this influence how he felt about your product? I think it might.

BAD QUESTIONS CAN MISLEAD

Many questions that work at one level in an organization fail at another, and the wrong type of question can sometimes produce misleading information. For example, let's say your investigation has uncovered the importance of shareholder value to your customer. You've heard this from the lips of both the CFO and CEO when they were responding to questions during a quarterly earnings report conference call.

Now I'm certain the CEO, COO and CFO would all agree that shareholder value was and is important; however, as you move down the org chart these macro issues lose their emotional resonance.

Is shareholder value important to the director who is short-staffed, subject to a hiring freeze, and doing the work of three people for his company? Wall Street and the investment community love head count reductions, and frequently greet news of one by boosting a company's share price, but is the overworked director as thrilled about these stock-boosting changes?

If you were to ask this director, "Is shareholder value important to you?" The answer you are likely to get is, "Of course its important." But this could be someone maintaining the company line. This director might fear his real opinion might somehow reach the C-level suite and become a dreaded CLM (Career-Limiting Move).

The problem with the question and its answer is the way it misleads. Imagine this director is the decision maker for your product and you base your presentation on this "need" you've uncovered, and how your product delivers the best shareholder value and return on investment of any product of its type. Will such a presentation, devoid of emotional power, cause a favorable buying decision? That is doubtful. In fact, such a presentation might stir up negative emotions of resentment since macro-issues, like shareholder value, are forcing your decision maker to work like a galley slave.

There is a way to avoid these questioning pitfalls and that is by taking the steps outlined below.

STEP ONE: DEVELOP THE CUSTOMER PROFILE

The first step in the process is to develop individual profiles of the decision maker and decision influencers. What are their jobs and responsibilities? What are their typical concerns? What are their biggest problems?

For example, if the Chief Information Officer (CIO) is a decision maker then you know, or can easily find out, that among his likely concerns are the security and stability of the network, cost reduction, productivity enhancement, and so on. If you are unfamiliar with their responsibilities and concerns, then the Internet can provide this information. Simply search "top CIO concerns" and you will get a mountain of feedback. You can filter this further by specifying the industry, the state, etc. If you've been working in the same field for a while, then your experience should enable you to fill out this profile.

Also, if your company has a CIO, try to get an hour of his time during lunch to ask him questions and understand his world from an emotional perspective. What does he fear? What does he think our CIO customers likely fear when they are purchasing our product, or a competitive product? What are his goals or hopes?

These conversations can produce priceless information. I remember speaking to the head of our company's IT department and finding out our CIO customers were fearful about making a purchase of a large system like ours, and then have it fail to produce any of the productivity gains they promised would occur. This fear was reinforced by the high turnover rate of CIOs at the time. This led us to put greater emphasis during presentations on our installation process, and how we would help them drive the necessary behavior changes in the end-users to produce the productivity gain.

Step one is completed when you develop a list of concerns and problems faced by this particular customer. A partial list of a CIO's likely concerns/interests might look like this:

1. Ensuring the network has the capacity to handle large amounts of traffic.
2. Protecting the security of the network.
3. New products should follow existing standards—be it a fire alarm system, security system, etc.—to prevent the addition of separate networks requiring their own back-up systems, maintenance schedule, etc.

One of these areas of concern could be a failed installation. If a customer has purchased a software program for their network that never delivered on its promise, and it was de-installed, then he will likely be interested in training programs, support, and so on.

You can add to your list:

4. De-installs.

5. Training programs that make de-installs less likely, etc.

It is important to find out industry specific concerns so you are able to show you understand their unique needs. For example, hospital CIOs may have specific needs centered on Electronic Medical Record development. Being conversant in these specific subjects, and asking insightful questions about them, can change a customer's perception of the salesperson. It can make him appear to be a member of the team, a consultant who is working toward solving their problems.

Also, issues specific to the organization they work for will have a major impact on their responsibilities and concerns. The CEO may have tasked the CIO with transformational goals driven by the innovative use of information to improve decision-making. One never knows how the leadership in an organization will give an enterprise a unique focus, but the salesperson needs to find this out.

STEP TWO: MATCH SOLUTIONS TO CONCERNS

We marry the primary benefits of the product we represent to the concerns of the customer in the second stage. You go down the list of their concerns and say, "For this concern we offer this solution. And for this concern we offer that solution." And down the list you go writing down the solutions that fit the best and are the most powerful.

For example, you determined protection against the occurrence of de-installs was a concern, so you develop a list of the way your product addresses this concern:

•   Your product has never been de-installed, while all competitive products have.

•   The reason for your success is the package of training that comes with the install. The hours allotted for training are 40% more than your next closest competitor.

STEP THREE: DEVELOP QUESTIONS

Next, we develop questions that validate the strength of these concerns. Let's return to the suspected concern about de-installs. It leads us to develop the following question:

Have you ever experienced a software de-install and is it a concern?

This question wants to discover if this is an area that either elicits a pained response or no response. If they have experienced a de-install, then it is likely they want to avoid going through it again. But they may try to conceal their emotional reaction to the question and simply offer a tight-lipped, "Yes. I've experienced a de-install."

The following is critical. The questions you have on a sheet of paper may not produce all of the information you need, but the follow-up questions typically do. Therefore, you do not go on to the next question until you understand how strong or weak their emotional response is to this question. You must continue to burrow deeper with potential questions like:

How did that process go for you?

Was it costly?

What went wrong?

If they answer, "I'd rather not relive that experience." Then you will know this was an emotional experience worth addressing during your presentation and that digging any deeper, at this time, will only generate negative feelings toward you.

I've found that in most instances customers are quite free to share their bad experiences, because they don't want to relive them in the future. Listening to your solution may provide them with a much-desired sense of relief.

Customers are also more likely to speak freely when you preface your questions with the following promise:

I understand you are going to be attending the presentation this Friday, is that correct? Great. To make this presentation relevant to you and your department, I'd like to ask you a few questions to find out what some of your concerns are. If I know what they are, then I can speak about how our product addresses these concerns.

For example, have you ever experienced a software de-install and is it a concern?

Note: I've stated the reason why I am asking him questions in a way that focuses on his benefit. If he answers my questions, then at least one of the long presentations he has to sit through will address some of his concerns. It's like saying, "Give me a moment of your time so that I don't completely waste your time on Friday."

Also, I don't ask his permission to ask questions. I don't ask if he has time to answer them right now—because this may be my only chance to ask them. Instead, I launch into the first question as a way of showing how they will be relevant to his concerns.

That said, if I see him fidgeting or looking at his watch, then I ask if there is a better time to conduct this brief survey. Someone who is visibly distracted is a bad candidate for questions. Their mind is elsewhere, perhaps on a meeting they are already late to attend. Since I want to create the mindset that I am a consultant who is part of their team, I cannot allow my behaviors to undermine this by acting like I don't value his time.

STEP FOUR: TEST THE SOLUTION'S ACCEPTABILITY

You've now discovered an emotionally hot area and you have a product solution that fits it. Why do I need to test whether or not they value our solution? It's our solution...what else am I going to present? The following example illustrates the importance of this step:

> There was a hospital trying to improve the patient's experience. Also, due to a nursing shortage, they were looking for ways to make nurses more productive and remove unnecessary steps.
>
> It just so happened that there was a perfect solution to their problem: A wireless phone network. When a patient called for help a phone-carrying technical assistant could answer to find out what was needed. The patient might say, "I need a blanket." Now the tech could go get the blanket and deliver it rather than walk to the room, find out what is needed, walk to get the blanket, and then walk back to the room. The patient's call would be answered more quickly, and the need was taken care of with fewer steps being taken. Patient satisfaction scores rise, unnecessary steps are removed... it's perfect!
>
> It's presentation time. You are so amped you can barely control yourself. You now remind the account of their goals, present your solution, and the nurses respond. "I don't want a phone to interrupt me when I am trying to take care of a patient." Another stirs up the emotion of fear: "What if the phone rings, it is a patient in distress, and I am changing a wound dressing? The patient dies, and the phone log shows I failed to answer their call, because I couldn't. Phone system? No way."

This is why you test a solution first. It can keep you from walking into a buzz saw. If you know the concerns your solution generates, you can either deal with them upfront, or focus on other solutions.

We return to the de-install example to show how this stage of the questioning is handled:

> We share your concern about de-installs. We are the only company in our space that has no de-installs and the reason why is we offer a comprehensive training program that makes de-installs far less likely. *Would you like me to cover that during the presentation?*

> He responds, "In detail. And I want you to explain to the people why it is critically important that they all participate in this training, because if they don't, we all lose."

The strength of the response let's you see how emotionally important the solution is. It also reveals how you will score a lot of points if you can "sell" the nursing staff on the value of the training to them and their departments.

FOLLOW-UP QUESTIONS AND NOTES

Follow-up questions are vital to the success of your consultative questioning. The first question sometimes generates a meaningful response, but we shouldn't be satisfied with it. For example, let's say you ask, "Have you ever experienced a software de-install and is it a concern?" And the CIO answers, "Yeah I've been through a de-install, and it got me de-installed. So I'd say it was important."

This is valuable information and, by itself, it might be all you need to craft a solution that wins the sale. But why not probe a little more deeply? The follow-up questions are often the ones that unlock the door to sales success. So you ask, "What's the worst thing about a de-install?"

The CIO answers:

> It's like throwing away hundreds of invested man-hours. Time is our most precious commodity and we will never get back any of that wasted time.

Memorable phrases from decision makers are like diamonds from a mine. These words are the product of enormous pressure and they are extremely valuable. Be sure you write down answers like this word for word, because when it comes time to present the product you can say the following:

> Our product has never been de-installed. None of our competitors can say this. If you choose our system, you won't need to worry about *throwing away hundreds of invested man-hours*. This is

critical, because *time is our most precious commodity*. And the time you lose from a de-install is time you *will never get back.*

The italicized words came directly from the CIO's mouth. As you repeat his words, you will see him furiously nodding his head up and down. It is like you are speaking directly to his soul. "He gets it!" this person's mind will shout. It will seem like you are reading his mind, because you are literally giving voice to his thoughts. When we speak a decision maker's own words back to an audience that they are a part of, it is as if we have publicly validated what they have believed for years. Is that emotionally powerful? Oh yes.

If a customer says something memorable and emotion-laden do not bring attention to it by saying something like, "That's great stuff." Or, "Do you mind if I use that." Simply write it down and use it during your next presentation.

FRAMING THE QUESTION

Let's say you have identified network security as an area of customer concern. Is it wise to ask, "Is network security important for you?"

No. This question is unfortunate in that it successfully targets a concern, but in a way that makes you look like you have no clue what his CIO-world is like. He might think, dismissively, "Of course it's important. Does this guy know anything?" And then he might say, "Network security is important to everyone," to mask his disdain ever so slightly.

It is important to frame questions in a way that reveals an understanding of their profession. Another way to ask the same question is, "You have to juggle many priorities. Is network security your highest priority, or does anything outrank it?"

FROM THE PARTICULAR TO THE GENERAL

By asking questions that reveal your understanding of the decision maker's world and their needs, you will create the perception that you are not a salesperson, but a consultant who is trying to uncover problems and implement solutions. With that mindset established the customer is more likely to share things openly with you. Now you can ask general questions designed to uncover emotionally important areas that your targeted questions may have missed. For example, "What do you most fear occurring to your company or to your department?"

I remember a hospital administrator telling me, "Losing one of our busiest surgeons to a competitive hospital. If he walks away, then $12 million in annual revenue walks away with him." Up until the time I heard that answer I'd never thought about giving emphasis to the way our system improved the satisfaction of surgeons and physicians throughout the hospital since it was a system used primarily by nurses. But after that exchange, physician satisfaction became a part of every presentation.

Another general question that they have probably never been asked by anyone before is, "What are the things that you do in your job that you enjoy the most, that you are most passionate about?" If you can uncover the sources of joy in someone's oftentimes joyless job, and show how your product allows them to tap into that area of passion, you will not only improve your chances of winning the customer's business, you will also be on your way to developing an important business friendship.

NO KARNAKS NEED APPLY

The late Johnny Carson used to perform a comedy sketch wherein he became Karnak the Magnificent. (His work, though long gone, can still be found on YouTube.) Karnak had the amazing ability to know the answer to any question before the question was asked. To demonstrate this power he would hold an envelope to his head. In the envelope was the question. He would then announce the answer to the question before opening the envelope. For example, he might say the following answer, "Catch 22." Then he would open the envelope and read the question, "What would the Dodgers do if you hit 100 pop flies?"

In sales, there are no Karnaks. The answer comes after the question, not before, and once we assume we know the answer to a given question, we are preparing ourselves to receive an unhappy surprise. I experienced this first hand in Napa Valley.

We visited a hospital and gave a presentation based on how our product helped retain nurses by supplying them with the resources they needed to meet the demands of their job. This presentation had delivered us many purchase orders. It was resonating with customers because the nursing shortage was real at the time, and causing concern among hospitals. So we kept banging that bell—nursing shortage, nursing shortage—until finally the nurse interrupted me and said, "We don't have a nursing shortage here. I've got a list of people who are waiting for openings so they can join us. I don't know what its like elsewhere, but this is Napa."

"Hey Karnak," I thought as I kicked myself, "there is no benefit, perceived or real, when you pitch a solution to a customer that they don't need."

I share this humbling story so that you might remember to never assume you know the answer to the unasked question. Karnak was a great entertainer, but a lousy salesperson.

CONCLUSION

The causes of the buying decision are emotional, and we are in the process of realigning everything we do in sales to reflect this understanding. These questions, often referred to as a "needs analysis," are no longer an attempt to find out what their business supposedly needs. Instead, it is an attempt to find out what emotionally moves decision makers the most powerfully.

Needs analysis has always been an important exercise, because one's needs have an emotional component. But we improve this analysis by applying our understanding of the emotional causes of the buying-decision-effect. Instead of trying to discover "needs," we search for emotions like hope, fear, and joy. Needs analysis does not do this by design. If it did, then some of the questions I've introduced, "What are your goals?" and, "What are you passionate about in your work?" would be questions that are routinely asked. But they aren't, and that is because we have tended to approach sales as if it was a rational process, when it is not.

The effectiveness of asking questions, differentiation, stories, or anything we say, are affected nonverbally by how we say it. In the next chapter we will look at the power of the tone of our voice, and how we can modify this nonverbal component to improve the impact of our verbal charisma.

17

THE POWER OF YOUR VOICE

VOCAL ACCOMMODATION

I realize some of the subjects I've covered have been a little odd. Well, things are about to get a lot weirder, because the subject of vocal accommodation is really strange.

When two people are talking their pronunciation, speech rate, pause rate, and vocal intensity or volume, becomes virtually the same. They mirror one another's speech and this occurs subconsciously. This is what is called vocal accommodation and many research studies support this phenomenon's existence.

When we speak the sound of our voice has several elements. Among them are overtones and undertones. These elements make our voice fuller and more pleasant. We might not hear them as separate elements of speech, but we do notice when they are missing.

Undertones make a voice rich and resonant and also are a part of vocal accommodation. It is a sound that is subconsciously heard and we will now experience them.

EXPERIENCING UNDERTONES

To experience what undertones are, take a deep breath into your belly and speak a well-known phrase in a low voice. It could be, "To be or not to be." When you say these words they will be accompanied by a low-grumbling noise.

To replicate this grumbling noise, make the sound, "Ahhhhhhhhhh," after taking a deep belly-breath. You are basically replicating the type of sound that accompanies your words.

Say the phrase, "To be or not to be," again, after a deep belly breath and in a low voice, and see if you can now hear and feel the undertone in your voice more clearly.

Finally, experience words without an undertone. Take a shallow breath and say, "To be or not to be," in a high-pitched, nasally voice. Can you feel and hear the difference? Did you notice how the rumbling sound that accompanied your words when spoken with a lower tone disappeared?

Research shows that a thin, nasally voice, the type lacking resonant undertones, were rated more negatively than those that had them. That's no big surprise, but this might be:

> … when lower frequency sound is eliminated in people's interactions, they're not as able to complete a task in as accurate a manner, even though they can hear it very crisply. There's just something about the interaction that they have with the other person that is not complete.[1]

The discomfort caused by a voice with no undertones explains why phone conversations can become tiresome. Phones diminish our undertones and it is one of the reasons why long phone conversations are typically unsatisfying.

LOW PITCH AND LEADERSHIP

When I say, 'I am a strong leader,' in a high-pitched, nasally voice, my tone betrays my words. It is another example of the nonverbal-verbal disconnect that reaffirms **Charisma Axiom # 4:**

> When our words say one thing, but our nonverbal behaviors say another, people tend to believe our nonverbal voice.

A lower pitch, or a deeper voice, confers a mantle of leadership on a person. They may or may not be effective leaders, but the power of their voice alone makes others perceive them to be leaders. Studying the

---

[1] Nick Morgan, *Power Cues: The Subtle Science of Leading Groups, Persuading Others, and Maximizing Your Personal Impact* (Boston: Harvard Business Review Press, 2014), pp. 122-123. The research of Sociologists Dr. Stanford Gregory and Dr. Stephen Webster of Kent State University is highlighted in this book.

speeches of around 800 male CEOs, researchers at Duke University and the University of California came up with these findings:

> CEOs with deeper voices managed larger companies and, as a result, made more money. They enjoyed longer tenures. A decrease in voice pitch of 22.1 Hz was associated with a $187,000 increase in annual salary.[2]

To put the 22.1 Hz in perspective, there is about a 44-48 Hz difference in pitch between an alto and a tenor.

Additional research by Dr. Gregory on presidential elections from 1960 to 2000 found the winners in every election were the candidates with the lower pitch frequency.[3] Leaders appear to have a tone that influences others in ways we might never expect.

NONCONSCIOUS SOUND

Now here is where things get even stranger. It appears that System 1 has eagle eyes that see what System 2 cannot see (remember the flashed words on the computer screen?), and can hear what System 2 cannot hear. Yes, System 1 has the ears of a dog.

Dr. Gregory states, "people who put out the right kinds of sound—*below the range of conscious human hearing*—become the leaders of most groups."[4]

He based this belief, in part, on research involving twenty-five interviews conducted by Larry King. King once hosted a TV show on CNN where he interviewed famous people, some of whom were quite powerful. Dr. Gregory used recordings of these interviews to see if lower-status people accommodated the low-frequency sounds of higher-status people.

The researchers generated a curve for each voice sample. They could then see whose curve changed shape to accommodate the other. Or, another way

---

[2] Mayew et al, (2013). Voice pitch and the labor market success of male chief executive officers. Evolution and Human Behavior, 34, 243-248. As we will cover in the text, there is about a 30 Hz difference between an alto and a tenor's voice, so 22.1 Hz is almost dropping one's pitch an entire vocal range.

[3] Gregory and Gallagher (2002). Spectral analysis of candidates' nonverbal vocal communication. Social Psychology Quarterly.

[4] Nick Morgan, *Power Cues: The Subtle Science of Leading Groups, Persuading Others, and Maximizing Your Personal Impact* (Boston: Harvard Business Review Press, 2014), p. 121. Emphasis mine.

of stating this is: The "dominant" person's voice changed less when they were speaking to someone whose voice accommodated theirs.

The interviews came from 1992, and the following table details some of the twenty-five people King interviewed and how they ranked in terms of vocal-accommodation dominance and deference. In the top nine of this table, King's voice quickly accommodated theirs. In the bottom three the guest's voice quickly accommodated King's.

This undertone accommodation is another System 1 operation that occurs automatically and quickly, in about the first two minutes of a conversation. Each person listens to the other's voice and then the follower subconsciously accommodates the leader.

A table showing the dominance and deference rankings of the top ten and the bottom three interviewees now follows.

Name of Guest	Factor 1 Dominance		Factor 2 Deference	
	Guest	Larry King	Guest	Larry King
Top Ten				
Mike Wallace	0.85	0.26	0.28	0.8
George H. W. Bush	0.85	0.18	0.27	0.89
Elizabeth Taylor	0.84	0.19	0.16	0.78
Ross Perot	0.82	0.18	0.03	0.51
Bill Clinton	0.81	0.35	0.28	0.67
Barbra Streisand	0.8	0.29	0.07	0.76
Sean Connery	0.71	0.56	0.6	0.67
Tip O'Neill	0.7	0.55	0.44	0.76
Mario Cuomo	0.6	0.32	0.55	0.77
Bill Cosby	0.59	0.81	0.36	0.38
Bottom Three				
Spike Lee	0.15	0.89	0.8	0.17
Robert Strauss	0.12	0.84	0.83	0.31
Dan Quayle	0.09	0.92	0.83	0.05

THE RANKINGS

There were two groups of people in the above table's top ten: Men who were accustomed to wielding power and speaking in public, and entertainers.

In the powerful men category was a sitting president, President Bush; a soon-to-be-president, President Clinton; a presidential candidate, Ross Perot, who as an entrepreneur built and sold a multi-billion corporation to GM; a former Speaker of the House of Representatives, Tip O'Neill; and a former governor noted for his oratorical gifts, Mario Cuomo. These were all men accustomed to wielding power and you would expect to see names like this ranking high in dominance.

Then there is the second group: media celebrities. Not only did they take up five of the top-ten slots, they also outranked Desert Storm's commanding general, Norman Schwarzkopf, and former President Jimmy Carter, in terms of dominance. That's impressive enough, but what makes this number of five top-ten finishers even more startling is this: There were only six media personalities in the twenty-five people who were studied.

So, who was the only one who failed to crack the top ten? Julie Andrews, whose beautiful, high-pitched soprano voice weighed in at number fourteen on the dominance list.[5]

What can account for this lopsided performance? What makes celebrities so dominant, and people so deferential toward them? One thing these media personalities all have in common is a well-trained voice. Not only are they trained in nonverbal behaviors like facial expressions and body language, they are also trained extensively in the use of their voice. It is another reason why they have such charismatic influence.

Also, note how high Elizabeth Taylor's dominance and deference scores were. They were higher than Perot's and Clinton's and two male actors as well. Based on interviews with Larry King during this time period, found on YouTube, you can hear how her voice was deep and resonant. This shows how women, who typically do not have voices as deep as men, can still develop a deeper, leadership voice that can compete with the most powerful male voice.

If you have any doubt about women being able to develop a deeper, leadership voice, then watch the YouTube video contrasting a high-pitched, dainty Margaret Thatcher with her later appearance as the UK's

---

[5] The interviewed people who were a part of this study, who do not appear in the above table, are now listed in order of their dominance starting with number eleven: Norman Schwartzkopf, Al Gore, Jimmy Carter, Julie Andrews, Daryl Gates, Gordon Sullivan, Lee Iacocca, George Mitchell, Henry Kissinger, Garrison Keillor, Jean Kirkpatrick, and Arthur Ashe. The bottom three then follow Arthur Ashe.

prime minister who was so aptly named the Iron Lady.[6] It is a useful film study in the nature of charisma. She was not born with powerful nonverbal behaviors. She acquired them. She went from being a warm, sweet-seeming woman—an appearance ill-suited for the rough-and-tumble world of politics—to a fierce lioness.

Through voice training Thatcher deepened the tone of her voice by 46 Hz. Again, 44-48 Hz separates an alto voice from a tenor's. Dropping the pitch of her voice by a full vocal range was quite an accomplishment.

Thatcher realized that if she was going to fulfill her political ambition and become Prime Minister, then she needed to outcompete all of the other power-hungry alpha males in her party, and become the dominant alpha, and that is what she became. Her voice went from sweet to fierce and her facial expression experienced a similar transformation. Armed with this nonverbal voice she got the UK to follow her transformational lead.

As Elizabeth Taylor and Margaret Thatcher show, when it comes to a leadership voice what is more important than gender is to have a trained voice, one that projects from the diaphragm, meaning it is supported by more air than a voice generated by shallow breathing in the chest. It is air that gives the voice its rich over- and under-tones.

Finally, with respect to the above table, when you consider the bottom of the dominance rankings, one name jumps out at you. Anyone familiar with Dan Quayle, who ranked dead last in dominance, will immediately say, "No surprise there." Quayle was President George H. W. Bush's Vice-President. He had a deer-in-the-headlights look on his face during interviews, and a voice lacking any authority whatsoever.

As Quayle shows, if we wish to project a more authoritative presence and lead others, then we need to develop a leader's voice. So, how do we develop this voice? Some exercises that enable you to do this now follow.

ESTABLISH A BASE LINE

Step one: Make a recording of your current speaking voice. Don't prepare for this recording in any way. Use your normal conversational voice. This will be your base line from which you will grow and improve.

---

[6] The YouTube video is entitled "Margaret Thatcher voice before/after" uploaded on October 20, 2011. Now, depending on your politics, her leadership could be viewed as either a good thing or a bad thing. I will make no such judgment on that topic. But I will say this: Love her or hate her, Lady Thatcher was a powerful leader.

EXERCISES: DIAPHRAGMATIC BREATHING

Next, practice diaphragmatic breathing, or belly breathing. While standing or sitting upright, inhale deeply into your belly three times in succession. Your first inhalation will fill up most of your belly with air. But there is room for more air, so you follow it with a second inhalation. This will almost top off the tank, and the third inhalation will barely be able to take in any more air. Hold your breath for two seconds and then slowly exhale.

This is a way to force air into your belly to overcome the muscular resistance that comes from unconscious tensing. Following the three-consecutive-inhalations exercise, simply take a few deep breaths into your belly. Breathe in deeply and slowly, pause for two seconds and slowly exhale.

Repeat this by performing the three- consecutive-inhalations exercise followed by a few deep breaths into the abdomen. This alternation is to stretch this breathing space, and then use it in a relaxed fashion. And if you do nothing else other than practice diaphragmatic breathing, and speaking after your belly is full of air, then you will still improve your voice. This is because more air equals richer undertones in your voice.

Another way to deepen your breathing is to combine stretching exercises with deep breathing. For example, while standing, with your arms at your side, slowly raise your left arm and at the same time arch your upper body to the right, leaning sideways. When you achieve the full stretch your left arm will be arched over your head. In this position breath deeply into your belly and you may feel the ribs on your left side expanding. After three breaths do the same thing while arching your upper body to the left with your right arm arched overhead.

EXHALATION

Once we can get air in, we can then focus on how to get the air out. After taking a full, deep, belly breath, tense your stomach muscles and slowly retract them squeezing out the air. Think of your stomach as moving backward toward the spine, and as it follows this mental command you will exhale the air in your stomach. This is designed to get you in control of the diaphragm's muscles.

It can be practiced virtually anywhere and should be practiced at several different times during the course of the day. You will not only benefit from developing a deeper, more resonant, leadership voice, you will also experience the de-stressing that deep breathing exercises deliver.

Stressed people are tense and this tension, over time, leads most people to breathing shallowly into their chest, instead of deeply into their belly. This is an ironic outcome, because breathing deeply is one of the fastest, best ways to reverse the stress response and calm down. In other words, deep breathing should never be a casualty of stress; stress should be a casualty of deep breathing.

OPENING THE CHANNEL

The next thing we need to do is use this life-giving air to project words. To help us do that we will turn to Patsy Rodenburg, a voice coach for many famous actors.[7] She teaches a wide variety of exercises but we will focus on three of them. They will enable us to relax the mouth, neck and throat, project sound, and then project words.

A much-studied relaxation technique involves vigorously tensing a muscle for about five seconds and then allowing it to relax. It is simple and very effective. So, to relax the muscles of the mouth, and surrounding muscles as well, you will scrunch up your facial muscles for about five seconds and then release the tension. Wait for about ten seconds, or until they feel as relaxed as possible, and then repeat this exercise two more times. This will help your jaw to relax and open completely, and this is necessary if you want to project sound more fully.

The next exercise works on opening your throat. With your lips closed and your teeth apart begin to smile "and as the smile widens, open the jaw as far as you can without any discomfort or force. Keep the smile in place—don't let it droop. This movement will automatically open the throat—the fundamental prerequisite of a free voice. This opening may be accompanied by a desire to yawn, but the yawn is a good sign as it indicates the throat has been opened. Do this five times."[8]

Next time you perform this exercise combine it with diaphragmatic breathing. Once you release the jaw, take a few deep breaths with your fully open throat. After experiencing this, read a short poem with the full support of your deep breath. The following quatrain from W.B. Yeats poem, "The Lake Isle of Innisfree," will do:

> I will arise and go now, and go to Innisfree,

---

[7] Rodenburg is the founder of the Voice Department at London's Royal National Theatre.

[8] Patsy Rodenburg, *The Second Circle: How to Use Positive Energy for Success in Every Situation* (New York: W. W. Norton & Company, 2008), p. 82

And a small cabin build there, of clay and wattles made;
Nine bean-rows will I have there, a hive for the honey-bee,
And live alone in the bee-loud glade.

REACH OUT WITH YOUR VOICE

A heightened energy level is a core component of charisma and the following exercises enabled me to experience the incredible energy of a free voice. This, in turn, energized not just my voice but me. It was an outcome I never anticipated. I hope you feel this energy as well because it will help motivate you to perform these exercises that at first may seem odd.

To project your voice look across the room and find a spot above your eye-line. This will be your voice's target. Your voice will be moving up and out of you.

First, project your breath to that point to feel this air that will be supporting your sound and then your words. Next, after taking a deep breath, project the sound "oooooooo" to that point across the room. Keep the sound constant and do not allow it to drop off. Then project the "ooooo" and turn it into an "ahhhh," or "oooooahhhhh."

When I project this sound I like to do it in the deepest voice possible, but never straining my voice by going deeper than my natural voice will allow. The goal is deepening your voice, not losing it.

The next exercise is intoning and it makes the voice stronger.

> Intoning is a sustained release of voice on one note, rather like a monotone chant. Intone this phrase: "The grey sea and the long black land" to a point above eyeline. Throw or push it if required.
>
> Repeat the phrase at least three times.
>
> Now start intoning the words and on the same breath move into speaking.
>
> This could take several attempts to achieve, but once done you will experience a free, powerful, and placed voice.[9]

The next step is to intone an entire poem instead of just one line. Then immediately follow this with reading the poem in a normal voice. Then intone it and read it normally again.

---

[9] Rodenburg, p. 85.

What I found most powerful about Rodenburg's intoning technique is the way it forces your voice to be resonant, rich in undertones. And again, the energy you will feel is palpable.

This exercise need take no more than ten minutes in the morning. It can then continue with your conscious effort to project a free and clear voice during the course of the day. After about a week of work re-record your voice and then compare it to your first recording.

VOICE DEEPENING

The best exercise for me to deepen my voice was singing songs in a deep voice. I would choose songs sung by men with deep voices and I would try to match them note for note, but again, never straining my voice. It was a fun exercise that allowed me to practice diaphragmatically projecting my voice and it seemed to me that I was producing a new, freer, fuller sound.

You may never know what it is like to experience your true voice until you do these exercises. You also may never get the chance to harness the power of the voice like those charismatic men and women who went before you—Winston Churchill, Martin Luther King, Jr., Margaret Thatcher, to name a few.

But why not try? Aided by the power of rich, resonant voices, the above three people changed the historical course of nations. Imagine the impact it might have on your sales and your ability to influence others.

There is one last step that we need to take. It involves redefining our role as salespeople and helping our customers make the emotional migration from fear to trust.

18

REDEFINING YOUR ROLE

A NEW ROLE FOR SALESPEOPLE

Many customers, if not most, initially distrust the majority of the salespeople they meet. Charisma helps overcome this distrust, but so does redefining our role. From hereon out, we need to think of ourselves as being consultants instead of salespeople, and then start acting like consultants. Like charisma, this redefined role helps reshape the way we are perceived by our customers.

We do this for sound psychological reasons. We stop selling in the traditional manner because people resist being sold. Selling can generate cognitive strain's vigilance and suspicion—"He just wants our money," the strained customer thinks—and can create an us-them relationship.

Our goal is to put our customers at ease, and we do this by leading them to buying decisions through our charisma, and by sharing our emotionally compelling, consultative solutions. There is no longer an us-them relationship because when we solve a customer's problems and remove issues causing pain, we become a valuable member of the customer's team.

THE EMOTIONAL MIGRATION

When you sell a big-ticket item as I did, I oftentimes found myself selling to the customer and to a consultant. These customers used consultants because they feared making a purchasing mistake. When a customer is buying a complex product or service—e.g., a telecommunications system, etc.—and it is outside their expertise, they will often hire a consultant to fill in this knowledge gap.

The fear that drives customers into the arms of consultants is real, because the price of a bad decision is high. For example, let's say I have a budget of $1 million for some much-needed telecommunications gear, and I buy a system that lasts one year. The short shelf life of my purchase was caused by my company's expansion, and the inability of my chosen system to expand with us. A year after spending $1 million, our company now has to spend another million, or more, to get a new system that will grow with them. Ouch!

When we realize the consultant's role is to remove fear from the decision-making process by addressing fears, and providing wise counsel to the decision maker, we begin to understand what a consultative salesperson's role should be.

Instead of "selling" the customer, the consultative salesperson's role is to help him make the emotional migration from fear (what if we make a bad decision?), to trust (your solution meets our wants and needs), to partnership (we've bought your product, it works the way you said it would and you're now a part of our team). Charisma plays a central role in this migration toward a partnership, because its magnetic quality makes the customer want this person on their team.

A customer's fears are not just product related. They also extend to the company and salesperson representing the product. The consultative sales approach knows it must address these fears to enable the emotional migration toward a satisfying partnership.

PRODUCT FEARS

As Apple, Inc. taught the world, consumers love simple, intuitive products. Therefore, Apple designs products that require no training manual. This design philosophy was a major factor in their becoming the most highly-valued company in the world.

It is likely that your product does not enjoy the benefit of Apple's brand recognition. So, even if you have a genuinely simple product (this is reality), the customer may still see it as being too complex (perception trumps reality).

When *you* look at your product you see something you are familiar with. This familiarity makes working with this product as natural and easy as breathing. But when *your customer* looks at your unfamiliar product he sees something alien, something requiring training and making his complex life at work even more so.

Complexity can generate feelings of unease and fear. With the exception of self-destructive people, no one seeks to complicate their life needlessly. Because of this, if there was one fear I always tackled head on, whether I was speaking with end-users or administrative decision makers, it was the fear of complexity.

There are many ways to demonstrate a product's simplicity, but the one I found to be the most effective was asking a room full of customers who the most technologically challenged member of their group was. Ask it with a smile and it becomes a fun game for them to decide, and it usually doesn't take long. The technologically challenged typically have a reputation that they are almost proud of. He will either raise his hand, or their colleagues will quickly point him out.

Next, I would ask this person, "Would you be kind enough to participate in a product demonstration? The reason why I am asking you is simple. Customers want simple, easy-to-use products. Salespeople live with their products, so they can always make a product look simple, even when it's not. But if I can get you to use this product without much training, then it probably is easy to use."

Then I motion to a chair and say, "Please." I've never had a customer say no, and I believe this is largely due to selling with charisma. It inspires trust and confidence, and the feeling of safety and security.

Every product has some complexity, but if it is well designed, then its basic functionality is straightforward. So walking a technophobe through the demo is not difficult. I would keep this part of the demonstration short and basic. I would also cover the tasks that they would likely perform several times a day or week. For example, how do you sign into the system and how do you sign out. Then, when this demonstration was finished, I'd ask his colleagues to give him a round of applause, and the mood of the room was brightened for the rest of the presentation.

There are other product fears and these are typically uncovered when we ask our custom-tailored questions. Whatever they are, they need to be addressed. But two fears that often get overlooked involve the relationship that a purchase entails.

Is your company reliable, ethical, and likely to be in business several years down the road?

Are you, the salesperson, ethical, reliable, and committed to giving excellent service. If you work for a bad company, or if you are a bad salesperson, then the product can be great but the customer experience can be one of unending pain and suffering.

COMPANY FEARS

Are you a small company competing against giants? When you work for a small company, and there are big-company alternatives, the spoken or unspoken fears are, "Do you have the resources and the wherewithal to sustain product development and stay current with this rapidly-changing world? And will you be around five years from now to service our purchase?"

Turn this fear on its head by making this perceived weakness a significant strength. I would tell customers the following:

> What name is synonymous with searching the Internet? Google. If you think back far enough, Google was once a tiny little gnat compared to Yahoo, Microsoft and AOL-Time Warner. But in the game of Internet search, it crushed its much larger competitors. Why? Because Google focused on this one thing, searching the Internet, and did it better than anyone else. Search technology became their core competency, and it wasn't the core competency of Yahoo, Microsoft and AOL-Time Warner.

> We are also small compared to our competitors, but we are totally focused on the system you are considering. It is our core competency. However, when you look at our much larger competitors you will find that this system doesn't even appear in their annual reports. I've done automated word searches of these reports and this product category is never mentioned. And why would it be? It fails to generate enough revenue to move the needle of their all-important stock price.

> So, it isn't a focus for them. It is not a part of their core competency. But it is what we do. Period. And that's why we are the best at it.

The above returns to the subject of differentiation. It is the art of comparing your product, company, etc., to your competitors, in a favorable way. In the above, we not only make our small size our strength, but their large size a great weakness. The message is: They pay this product line little attention because it is so insignificant to them.

Also, note how I repeated the phrase "core competency." This underscores how we need to use the lessons we've learned about verbal charisma. This phrase made our focus a strategic strength, helped diminish concerns about our size, and cast shade on our larger competitors.

SALESPERSON FEARS

One of the biggest fears a customer can have is also the easiest one to control. If they do not know you, they may distrust you and question everything you say. Therefore, to establish a bond of trust follow this simple set of rules:

1. Radiate nonverbal charisma. It subconsciously communicates the message, "I am trustworthy." By itself, a salesperson's charisma is often enough.

2. Always be honest in what you do or say. Misrepresentations can cause irreparable damage to a relationship.

3. The customer doesn't care to know you until they know you care. Make an emotional commitment to always be there for the customer. If they need something—information, a part, some troubleshooting help—fill this need as fast as possible. If they call you and you cannot answer, then make sure you return their call in minutes not hours. This powerfully communicates to System 1 that they are the center of your universe.

4. Invest the time it takes to understand their world. Consultants do this when they are working on a project for a client.

5. Never be afraid to admit you do not know an answer to a customer's question. To be trusted requires a degree of honesty that is self-evident. However, it is up to you to get that answer for them ASAP.

6. Some salespeople use their strong relationships with customers to charge them the highest prices. They do this because they believe they can get away with it, and many do. But if you want to develop a genuine, trusting relationship, then price your product in a way that would stand up to your customer's examination of your books. Be profitable, but don't gouge.

7. Finally, differentiate your product. Though this is counterintuitive, it builds trust.

HUMOR

Trust. The word has a heavy connotation like the word *stolid*. But being relentlessly serious is no way to build a strong relationship. Customers will find ways to avoid the company of someone who is no fun to be around. So one of the ways to lighten the mood, and grow closer to a customer, is to use humor. It can even be built into your sales process.

We had a VP of Manufacturing who looked menacing. He was massive. It was rumored he had a neck, but the way his head fused to his torso proved the rumor was false. His head sported a Prussian buzz cut. His piercing blue eyes had an intensity that would have made him a great interrogator. And at every opportunity, I would ask him to lead the plant tours.

He would appear in the room where we conducted our presentations and would quietly stand off to the side and look menacing. He wasn't trying to look intimidating, he just did. I would then say, "I'd like to introduce our VP of Manufacturing. Some people are hired for their competence. Others are hired for their looks. You see this when you go to conventions where manufacturers show their gear. They always have face-guys and face-girls at their booths. Our VP of Manufacturing is a face guy."

Though I had said this many times, he would always smile and erupt in laughter—the menacing look would melt away—and he'd say, "Yeah, I'm a face guy." Then he would follow it up with a jab at me, "Salespeople. What are you going to do? Are you folks ready for our plant tour?" The customers immediately took a liking to him and the tour was always a success. Again, humor is a wonderful spice that can set a positive tone for an experience.

COMPETENCE INSPIRES TRUST

If a detailed process is in place, then make sure you find the answers to these questions:

1. What are the stages of their competitive bidding process and the dates?
2. Who is running the process, and is this person my primary point of contact?
3. Are there any special rules, like disqualifying a vendor if they try to speak to members on the decision-making committee?
4. How will the decision be made? For example, will a committee make it immediately after the final presentation?

5. Will there be site visits to see the actual product/service in use?
6. Will there be plant tours?
7. How many presentations will be required and how long will they be?

Once you have the answers, it is important that each step is prepared for and handled in a competent manner. If, for example, you bungle a site visit, or fail to submit requested information by the deadline, then you are damaging the bond of trust you are trying to form. We tend to trust reliable, competent people, and this is why it is critical to master the entire complex-sales process.

ALWAYS ADVANCE THE SALES PROCESS

It is easy to get lost in the details of a complex sale. One of the simplest tools to help manage one or more projects is to make sure each one has a next step and a date. Complex sales are advanced by increments and, until it is closed, it is easy to lose sight of the fact that there are concrete interim steps you can take to keep advancing the sale.

This means that until the sale is closed, and the customer is in-serviced and satisfied, you will always have a next step with a date attached to it. If your manager is not asking you what the next step and date is for an important sales opportunity, then you need to be asking yourself.

Even the final stages of a large sale require attention. Let's say you've just finished your final presentation along with your competitors, and the word from the committee is they will get in touch with you in one week with the information regarding who has won the bid. Your next step and date might be to handwrite on nice stationery a note of thanks to all who attended, and to let them know you are available at all times to answer any lingering questions they may have.

Once the note is mailed, your next step and date is to call the customer the day after the decision was to be announced, if an announcement was not made. This is important. The last thing you want to experience is losing the sale to a salesperson who is more persistent than you during a time when a dithering customer was indecisive.

If I am the only salesperson who fails to follow up with the customer, then it will look like I am not hungry for their business, and will probably not pay much attention to them once the deal is closed. It could be something this small and simple that neutralizes weeks or months of work. And it is so easy to overlook this unless you have a next step and a date.

CUSTOMERS FOR LIFE

With charisma, you will magnetically draw people into your sphere of influence. Now comes the most satisfying aspect of a sales career, namely, the development of emotionally satisfying and meaningful relationships.

Those outside of sales might scoff at this notion and say, "How can a salesperson's relationship to a customer be real when their top priority is to sell them a product? It is 'fake' real. You make nice to people to make a buck."

For some salespeople this characterization is accurate, but not for the world's best who develop customers for life. I've known them to counsel customers to not buy their product for a particular use because it will not enable them to achieve their specific goal. The end result is they temporarily lose one sale but they strengthen a trusting relationship. They demonstrate how they put the customer first and this puts them on the path to having a customer for life.

Imagine the alternative result. Let's say a salesperson supported their customer's decision to buy a flawed-product-solution. Then, six months later, after this product continually failed to deliver on its promise, what would happen to their relationship? It might be damaged beyond repair. The salesperson would now be seen as someone who was willing to make a buck at their expense.

When a customer finds a salesperson who they can partner with, they cling to them, fight for them, fend off competitive threats, because they know that what they have is rare, rarer than it should be.

The evidence that these relationships are real and meaningful is provided by the customer's response to a beloved—yes, beloved—salesperson's departure. Perhaps they retire, or accept a position with another company that calls on a different set of customers. In such cases, their customers are genuinely upset when this time of parting arrives. They are losing a trusted ally who bailed them out of jams, working tirelessly for them—over weekends if required—and uncomplainingly.

This is the person who helped guide them in buying decisions even when it meant steering them to a product other than his own. He also in-serviced staff members to make sure his system was adopted. He had a desk to work at when he arrived and was viewed as one of the customer's advisors. He was a part of the team and earned this position in dozens of ways.

Smart companies cherish these types of salespeople. They produce growth, year after year. When they introduce management to their customers these salespeople are almost embarrassed by the praise they receive from their customers. Statements are made like, "You'd better take care of him, because he is the only reason why we are doing business with you." And they are not joking. I've seen many accounts drop a company's products when they downsize and cut top salespeople.

FINAL WORDS: THE KEY TO SUCCESS

Your ability to sell with charisma does not depend on the degree of charisma you now possess. Clients of mine who were completely lacking in charisma became undeniably charismatic in days, and you can too.

But there might be one obstacle standing in your way. It stands in the way of people who know they need to exercise, but year after year fail to do so, and that is: Motivation and discipline. People who lack this will not perform these exercises that made my charisma-deficient clients so charismatic. They were highly motivated and disciplined and were richly rewarded for performing these charisma-producing exercises.

If there are too many exercises for you to handle, then focus on these two: Visualization and positive self-talk. Perform them at the same time to save time, but the bottom line is this:

> It does not take a lot of effort to become more charismatic, but it does require the drive and discipline to perform these exercises on a regular basis over the course of a week or less.

After all, we are talking about reprogramming System 1 and this takes some time and effort. But I promise you that it will be worth the effort, because charisma's exercises strengthen the mind, make the heart more compassionate toward others, and keep the body healthy.

It also touches upon one of the central things we do as human beings: communicate. Charisma is about making our communication as powerful and influential as possible.

Companies look for people who are effective communicators. Once you master the art of selling with charisma, you will be communicating at a level that most companies have yet to imagine.

www.ingramcontent.com/pod-product-compliance
Lightning Source LLC
Chambersburg PA
CBHW072006040426
42447CB00009B/1512